D1503593

"If you can believe the holy, rig[...]
all really cares about you and wa[...]
believe he wants *you* to love, as well. Phil Ryken has written a dangerous book. Drink in these thoughts, pore over these pages, but please do not keep this to yourself."

Chris Fabry, Host, *Chris Fabry Live!*; author, *Every Waking Moment*

"I wish I could say that I read *Loving Jesus More* with joy, but I didn't. I read it with grief. It exposed once again how weak and fickle my love for Jesus really is. Sadly, beneath my theological knowledge and biblical literacy is a heart that is still prone to wander. But Ryken didn't leave me with a better understanding of what it means to love Jesus and the pain of acknowledging that I love him less. No, this book drips with the love of Jesus for me—love that is constant even when it is not reciprocated. This book balances the shocking honesty of the gospel with its glorious hope. I'm thankful for the surgery done on me through this book, and I think you will be too."

Paul David Tripp, President, Paul Tripp Ministries; author, *What Did You Expect? Redeeming the Realities of Marriage*

"Phil Ryken has taught us about loving Jesus more by going deep to the truth of the Bible, by helping our hearts to be stirred up by Jesus's love for us, and by being direct and practical about loving the Lord and his church."

Joseph "Skip" Ryan, Chancellor and Professor of Practical Theology, Redeemer Seminary; author, *That You May Believe and Worship: Beholding the Beauty of the Lord*

"At the heart of Christianity is a simple passion: *love for Jesus*. Everything flows from this passion. And yet for most, love for Jesus is elusive. In *Loving Jesus More* Phil Ryken gives you a path to follow that will fan that passion into a flame."

Paul E. Miller, Director, seeJesus; author, *A Loving Life*

LOVING
JESUS
MORE

Select List of Other Crossway Books by Phil Ryken

Kingdom, Come!

Grace Transforming

Christian Worldview: A Student's Guide

Loving the Way Jesus Loves

King Solomon: The Temptations of Money, Power, and Sex

Justification

Is Jesus the Only Way?

Our Triune God: Living in the Love of the Three-in-One
    (co-author)

LOVING JESUS MORE

PHIL RYKEN

WHEATON, ILLINOIS

Loving Jesus More

Copyright © 2014 by Philip Graham Ryken

Published by Crossway
        1300 Crescent Street
        Wheaton, Illinois 60187

Cover design: Erik Maldre

First printing 2014

Printed in the United States of America

Trade paperback ISBN: 978-1-4335-3408-9
ePub ISBN: 978-1-4335-3411-9
PDF ISBN: 978-1-4335-3409-6
Mobipocket ISBN: 978-1-4335-3410-2

Library of Congress Cataloging-in-Publication Data

Ryken, Philip Graham, 1966–
   Loving Jesus more / Phil Ryken.
     pages cm
   Includes bibliographical references and index.
   ISBN 978-1-4335-3408-9 (tp)
   1. God (Christianity)—Worship and love. 2. Jesus Christ.
3. Spirituality—Christianity. 4. God (Christianity)—Love.
I. Title.
BV4817.R95   2014
231'.6—dc23   2014005708

Crossway is a publishing ministry of Good News Publishers.

VP		24	23	22	21	20	19	18	17	16	15
15	14	13	12	11	10	9	8	7	6	5	4	3	2

Leroy Patterson
Victor Gordon
Stephen Kellough

*We give thanks to God always for all of you, . . .
remembering before our God and Father your
work of faith and labor of love and steadfastness
of hope in our Lord Jesus Christ.*

1 Thessalonians 1:2–3

Contents

Preface

Writing teachers usually advise their students to "write what they know." They say this because the best books come from authors who have intimate personal experience with the subjects they write about.

To tell the truth, I do not always follow this advice, and this book about loving Jesus is a good example. When it comes to loving Jesus, I'm no expert. Just ask my family, or maybe the people who work with me every day. So I am writing what I *don't* know—or don't know as well as I should.

Here is another truth, however: I want to love Jesus more. I also want the campus I lead to be saturated more and more with divine affection. I want it to be common for us to express love for Jesus—not just when we worship in chapel, but also when we share a meal in the dining hall, play the last movement of a symphony, score the winning goal in a soccer match, or talk over the day's events with friends.

One of the ways I grow the most spiritually is by teaching the Bible. So during the 2012–2013 academic year I decided to preach a series of messages on loving Jesus more—not because I am a very good lover, but because I wanted to learn, and help my students learn, too.

Those chapel messages have been edited here for a wider audience. I am grateful to Lynn Wartsbaugh and Lydia Brownback, especially, for their help in getting this book ready for publication.

I am dedicating what I have written to Chaplain Pat, Chaplain Vic, and Chappy K—three Wheaton College chaplains whose loving encouragement in Christian discipleship, faithful ministry in the Word of God, and reverent leadership in public worship have been a blessing to my life and ministry.

1

Where Love
Comes From

The goal of this book is to help people grow more in love with Jesus.

How important is it for us to pursue this goal? At the beginning of his classic devotional text, *The True Christian's Love to the Unseen Christ*, the Puritan Thomas Vincent wrote:

> Love to Christ being so essential unto true Christianity, so earnestly looked for by our Lord and Master, so powerfully commanding in the soul and over the whole man, so greatly influential on duty, I have made choice to treat this subject of love to Christ, and my chief endeavor herein shall be to excite and provoke Christians unto the lively and vigorous exercise of this grace of love into the Lord Jesus Christ, of which incentive there is great and universal need.[1]

To make the same point more simply, there is hardly anything we need more in the Christian life than more love for Jesus. But this is a daunting challenge. Part of the challenge is personal: Will we really love Jesus more as a result of reading this book? But behind this lies the even greater challenge of comprehending God's love for us, which is the true and ultimate source of all love for him. How can anyone do justice to the great love of God?

A.W. Tozer wrestled with this question in *The Knowledge of the Holy*, where he described the love of God "as an incomprehensibly vast, bottomless, shoreless sea." Tozer observed that if we are going to understand God, "we must try to speak of his love," for God is love. Yet this is difficult for even "the loftiest eloquence," as he explained:[2]

> All Christians have tried [to explain God's love] but none has ever done it very well. I can no more do justice to that awesome and wonder-filled theme than a child can grasp a star. Still, by reaching toward the star the child may call attention to it and even indicate the direction one must look to see it. So as I stretch my heart toward the high shining love of God someone who has not before known about it may be encouraged to look up and have hope.[3]

As we consider God's love for us in Jesus, which is the source of our love for him, we are "reaching for the stars." But even if we are not able to "grasp how wide and long and high and deep is the love of Christ" (Eph. 3:18–19 NIV), at least we can point toward it and say, "See, there it is: the love of God in Jesus Christ." And the more we see this love, the more our hearts will grow in affection for our Savior.

Loving Jesus Less

I have given this book the simplest title I could: *Loving Jesus More*. But this title presupposes yet another problem. If we say that we want to love Jesus *more*—or that we ought to love him more, whether we want to or not—then we are admitting that we do not love Jesus as much as we should. Logically, the only people who can love Jesus *more* are people who love him *less*. And unfortunately this is true for all of us. Our love is limited—not just for one another, but also for Jesus.

When we open the Scriptures, we discover that we are not alone in this limitation (which, in a way, is encouraging). The failure of God's people to love their God is one of the most pervasive themes in the story of salvation.

We see this all the way through the Old Testament. The story of the children of Israel is really a love story. God has a heart full of love for his people, which he proves over and over again by what he says and what he does. "I have loved you with an everlasting love," God declares. "Therefore I have continued my faithfulness to you" (Jer. 31:3).

The children of Israel were called to respond to this everlasting affection by loving God in return. Every day devout believers would confess their love for God in heart, soul, and strength (see Deut. 6:4–5). Yet they repeatedly failed to live up to their promises by turning their hearts against God.

One of the ways that God confronted this failure was by styling himself as a wounded lover. His passion smolders on the pages of the Old Testament. Understand that God's romance with his people was a spiritual marriage. So when their hearts grew cold, it was the ultimate betrayal. The imagery that the Old Testament uses to describe this marital breakdown is shocking. On occasion God compared Israel to a groom who cheated on his wife, or to a virgin who became a prostitute (e.g., Ezekiel 16). In the book of Jeremiah God actually files for divorce on the grounds of spiritual adultery (see Jer. 2:1–3:5). But he never gives up on his love covenant with his people. To exemplify his undying love, he tells his prophet Hosea to return to a wayward woman and take her to be his wife all over again.

We see something similar in the New Testament, where the followers of Christ often fall out of love. When Jesus warned his disciples that the hearts of many would grow cold (Matt. 24:12), he knew what he was talking about. The first generation of the church was also the first generation to love Jesus less. By the end of the New Testament, John was already warning the first Christians in Ephesus that they had forsaken their first love (Rev. 2:4).

Notice that in every case the people who struggle to stay in love with God are people who have experienced his blessings directly. The children of Israel had every reason to love God. He had delivered them from slavery, conquered their enemies, and established their kingdom. Yet even in a land of milk and honey, they fell out of love with God. Or consider the church in Ephesus, which was planted by the apostle Paul, led by Pastor Timothy, and later led by the apostle John—the evangelist of God's love. Despite this exceptional care, the Ephesians succumbed to spiritual entropy; their hearts grew cold.

All Out of Love

What has happened to your love for Jesus? Maybe you are falling more in love with him all the time. Jerry Trousdale has written about the way this is happening across the Muslim world in his book *Miraculous Movements*, which has a thrilling subtitle: *How Hundreds of Thousands of Muslims Are Falling in Love with Jesus*. This is a marvelous way to describe the Christian life, as a romance with Jesus.

According to Trousdale, it is happening all over the Muslim world: people who grew up reading the Koran are falling in love with Jesus. He tells the story of a man he calls "Zamil"—a successful businessman, prominent citizen, and leader in his local mosque. One night Zamil had a dream in which Jesus appeared to him and claimed to be the Light of the World. Zamil was blinded by the light, and when he awoke, he was unable to see. Soon he came into contact with local Christians, heard the gospel, and gave his heart to Jesus. Naturally, he prayed that God would restore his sight. But God did not answer that prayer, or protect him from the jealousy of family members who disowned and dispossessed him. Yet the Holy Spirit gave Zamil such a passionate love for Jesus that he could not keep the gospel to himself. Zamil went to nearby villages and started preaching the good news of Jesus and his love. When Trousdale met him two years later, the blind evangelist was already planting his eighth church![4]

When we are truly in love with Jesus, we will overcome any obstacle to advance his kingdom. Yet it is all too easy for our affections to move in the opposite direction. Thomas Vincent gave his readers a simple way to test the extent of their love for Jesus. "When you leave Christ quite out of your discourse," he wrote, "it shows that you have not an abundance of love to him because, out of the abundance of the heart, the mouth will speak of their riches. Such as have much love to pleasures will be often speaking of that subject; such as love their friends much will be often speaking and commending them when they are in company. And when you speak but little of Christ, it is a sign that you love Him but little."[5]

As we look back, we may well realize that there was a time when we were more in love with Jesus than we are today. Maybe that time was when we first came to Christ in repentance and faith. We were so happy to receive the free gift of eternal life that Jesus was the sole object of our affection. Or maybe we felt more that way later on. God helped us, healed us, rescued us, or provided for us, and we could only respond with loving gratitude. Our hearts were moved in worship or humbled by the amazing gifts we had received, and it was natural to say, "I love you, Jesus, for loving me the way you do."

Perhaps that moment has long since passed. Now life is filled with so many affections—all the other things we say that we "love": the latest video game, our beverage of choice, a favorite hobby, the hometown team. We still love Jesus to some extent, but he's like the old backpack that we're comfortable with but no longer excited about. Or maybe he is like the crush we had back in high school, and now it's hard to remember how we could have been so infatuated. If we are totally honest, we have to admit that we love our Savior less.

Love's Channel

If we are not content with loving Jesus less, but actually want to love him more, then we must learn how and where to get that love. What is the channel for receiving the love that will enable us to grow in our love for Jesus?

At first the answer may seem obvious. And it *is* obvious. We know that "God is love" (1 John 4:8). Love is one of his defining attributes. We also know that "we love because he first loved us" (1 John 4:19). So, of course, God is the source of all our love, including our love for God himself.

We can be more specific, however. In Romans 5, as Paul begins to apply the saving doctrine of justification by faith, he says something significant about the origin and the channel of God's affection:

> Therefore, since we have been justified by faith, we have peace with God through our Lord Jesus Christ. Through him we have also obtained access by faith into this grace in which we stand, and we rejoice in hope of the glory of God. Not only that, but we rejoice in our sufferings, knowing that suffering produces endurance, and endurance produces character, and character produces hope, and hope does not put us to shame, because God's love has been poured out into our hearts through the Holy Spirit who has been given to us. (Rom. 5:1–5)

Here Paul simply is spelling out the implications of our justification. By faith in Christ we stand righteous before God and have confidence to face the coming judgment. Part of the proof for this justifying grace is our present experience of the love of God. The apostle then proceeds to explain that the love of God is the love of Calvary—the love Christ showed to us when we were still sinners by dying for us on the cross (Rom. 5:8).

But notice the channel of that love. The love we have within us—the love that is poured into our hearts—comes through the third person of the Trinity: "God's love has been poured into our hearts *through the Holy Spirit* who has been given to us" (Rom. 5:5; cf. Rom. 15:30). Whatever love we have was put there by the Spirit of God. God has placed his love into our hearts specifically through the delivery of the Holy Spirit.

When Paul tells us that the Spirit gives us the Father's love, he is not drawing a sharp distinction between the love of these two divine persons. The love of the Father and the love of the Spirit are one and the same love, for there is no division of affection within the Godhead. Yet this verse does highlight the distinctive role of the Holy Spirit in communicating the love of God.

People sometimes wonder exactly what the Holy Spirit does. We know who the Father is because most of us have fathers of our own, or know other fathers. We know the Son because we read his story in the Gospels. But who is the Holy Spirit? What does the Spirit do? This is part of the answer: the Holy Spirit puts God's love into our hearts. The great American theologian Jonathan Edwards said that the Spirit's office is "to communicate divine love to the Creature." When the Spirit does this, Edwards went on to say, "God's love doth but communicate of itself."[6] In other words, in giving us the Holy Spirit, God gives us his own love.

Consider how amazing this is, and how necessary. God does not expect us to love him with our own puny love, which is so feeble and fickle. Instead, he invites us to love him back with the love that he gives. God has a generous heart. He gives us so much of his love that we have enough left over to use for loving him. As Timothy Dudley-Smith has written in one of his gospel hymns:

Safe in the shadow of the Lord,
Possessed by love divine,
I trust in him, I trust in him.
And meet his love with mine.[7]

William Temple, who served as the Archbishop of Canterbury during World War II, illustrated the inward work of the Holy Spirit by drawing an analogy to William Shakespeare. "It is no good giving me a play like Hamlet or King Lear," Temple said, "and telling me to write a play like that. Shakespeare could do it—I can't. And it is no good showing me a life like the life of Jesus and telling me to live a life like that. Jesus could do it—I can't. But if the genius of Shakespeare could come and live in me, then I could write plays like his. And if the Spirit could come into me, then I could live a life like His."[8]

This is what the Spirit does to enable us to live with Christlike love: he comes right inside us, and once he is there, he fills us with the love of God. Jesus told his disciples that he wanted them to have his Father's love within them (John 17:26; cf. 1 John 4:16). The way he fulfills his promise and accomplishes this purpose is by sending us the Holy Spirit. Part of the Spirit's ongoing work is to produce the fruit of love in the life of every believer (see Gal. 5:22). Whenever we look into our hearts and find even a small measure of true love for Jesus, this must be the work of God the Holy Spirit.

Getting the Spirit

This assumes, of course, that we have the Spirit to begin with. We will never love Jesus at all without the third person of the Trinity. If he is the channel of God's love, then in order to love Jesus more we need to have the Holy Spirit. So as we examine our hearts, we need to ask whether we have truly received the Holy Spirit. Do I have the Spirit in my life? Have I experienced his regenerating power? Am I born again?

The unmistakable sign of the Spirit's presence is faith in Jesus Christ. This is what the Holy Spirit comes into our lives principally to do: give us faith and love for Jesus Christ.

Listen to the way that one former imam testified to the Spirit's power. It started with a conversation he had one morning with his grandfather, who was also an imam.[9] The two men were discussing the death of Mohammad. According to the Qur'an, when Mohammad was dying, his daughter Fatima said, "Father, you are dying, but where are you going from here and what will happen to us?" All Mohammad could say in response was, "Ask me anything from my wealth, but I cannot save you from Allah's punishment." Then he said, "By Allah, though I am the apostle of Allah, yet I do not know what Allah will do to me." The prophet himself was uncertain of receiving mercy.

The former imam remembered this conversation later, when he was reading the New Testament. A Christian missionary had challenged him to read the Gospel of John. He

23

was happy to do this so that he could discover the Bible's mistakes and then argue with the missionary. But as he was reading, the man encountered the words of Jesus in John 14: "I am going to the Father. I go to prepare a place for you. And if I go and prepare a place for you, I will come again and receive you to Myself; that where I am, there you may be also. And where I go you know, and the way you know."

Immediately the man ran to his grandfather and asked him again what Mohammad had said when he was dying. After his grandfather recited the Qur'an, the man said, "Grandfather, look at Jesus. He said he was going to his Father and he would prepare a place for his followers, and after that he will come back. But Mohammad doesn't know where he is going, so which one would you follow?" From that moment on, the imam started to follow Jesus. By the power of the Holy Spirit, he fell in love with the Savior who actually knows where he is going, and has promised to take us there with him.

Understand that once you have the Holy Spirit in your life, he may not call very much attention to himself. The Spirit has such a strong desire to show us the Son that he is almost shy. Maybe this is true of each person of the Trinity, because they are always directing attention to one another. The Father wants to glorify his beloved Son (e.g., Matt. 3:16–17). The Son seeks to honor his Father (e.g., John 17:1). And when the Son promised to send us the Spirit, he boasted that the Spirit would enable us to do even greater works than he did (John 14:12–17)! The Father, the Son, and the Holy Spirit are never narcissistic, but always give one another the glory. There is mutual admiration within the Godhead.

The Spirit's love for the Father and the Son explains why the Spirit sometimes seems rather shy. But even if the Spirit does not call very much attention to himself, he is unmistakably there. Whenever we are impressed with the truth of God's Word, or convicted of our sin, or convinced that Jesus is the Christ, or motivated to worship, or empowered to serve other people, the Holy Spirit is at work. We know for sure that he is at work whenever we have true love for Jesus, because the Spirit is the channel of God's love.

Keeping in Step with the Spirit

Once we have the Holy Spirit, it is vitally important to leave our lives open to his influence. If we want to love Jesus more, and if the Spirit is the source of that love, then we should do everything we can to keep the channel of his grace wide open.

The Bible gives some very specific instructions about our response to the Spirit. It tells us some things we should be sure to do, and also some things we should be careful *not* to do. On the positive side, we are told to "walk by the Spirit" (Gal. 5:16) and "keep in step with the Spirit" (Gal. 5:25). This principally means following the words that the

Holy Spirit has revealed in the pages of Holy Scripture. But it also means following the leading of the Spirit through his inward work in our mind, heart, and conscience.

When the Spirit speaks, be ready to listen. Learn how to hear his voice—not so much as an audible word (although if the Spirit chooses to speak that way, that is up to him), or as some sort of infallible indicator for daily decision-making (don't go around saying, "God told me to do this," or worse, "God told me to tell *you* to do this"), but as the gentle guide who is constantly drawing us toward true spiritual life. When the Spirit prompts us to pray, we should pray. When the Spirit gives us the impulse to share our faith, we should give someone the gospel. Believers who follow the inner leading of the Holy Spirit grow dynamically and work effectively for the kingdom of God.

On the negative side, the Bible tells us not to "quench" (1 Thess. 5:19) or "grieve the Holy Spirit of God" (Eph. 4:30). The Bible talks about quenching the Spirit in the context of prayer, worship, and the ministry of God's Word (see 1 Thess. 5:16–21). We quench the Spirit whenever we sense him leading us to do something and then fail to follow through. We know we should pray, but it seems like too much work, so we skip it instead. Our conscience is troubled by sin, but we never actually tell Jesus that we're sorry for what we have done, or failed to do. We sense an opportunity to share the gospel, but we are not sure what to say, so we change the subject to something trivial. These are all ways of quenching the Spirit.

It is also possible to grieve the Spirit, which we do whenever we persist in rebellious sin. After all, the Spirit is a *Holy* Spirit, and therefore as he lives in us, he wants us to be holy. The context in which the Bible tells us not to grieve the Spirit is noteworthy. "Let no corrupting talk come out of your mouths," the Scripture says. "Let all bitterness and wrath and anger and clamor and slander be put away from you, along with all malice" (Eph. 4:29, 31). Bad language, hate speech, and words that tear people down grieve the Spirit of God.

All of this may help to explain why we are not falling more in love with Jesus. When we do not turn to God in prayer or encourage people in the gospel, then we quench the Spirit. When we curse God or speak against other people, we grieve the Spirit. As a result, we choke off the channel of God's love.

The Bible warns of these dangers in order to encourage God's full work in our lives. Rather than quenching or grieving the Holy Spirit, Jesus wants us to open our hearts to his love. There is still hope for us to grow in love because God does not give up on us. How amazingly gracious God is to give us his Spirit—the Spirit who even now is striving inside us to grow us in the love of God. God knows that we are not very good lovers. So by the Spirit he has poured his infinite love into our hearts.

A simple illustration may help to show how this works. When my son Jack was ten, he spent part of his summer at Honey Rock camp in northern Wisconsin. When he came back home, he amazed us by presenting a gift to each and every member of the family—all six of us. Each gift had been handmade at the craft shop. Each gift was unique, and carefully chosen for the recipient. When I asked Jack where he had managed to get the materials to make these gifts, he told me that he paid for his supplies with money from his camp account. Suddenly I realized that I had been the major financial investor in Jack's craft-making, gift-giving enterprise. Yet this realization did not diminish the heartwarming expression of the boy's love for his mother and father, or his brother and sisters. He took what he had been given and turned it into an expression of his love.

It is the same with the loving worship and heartfelt service that we offer to Jesus. God has put his love into our lives by pouring his Spirit into our hearts. So when we desire to love Jesus more, we are not limited to loving him out of our own small affection, but can love him with the abundant love that he freely gives.

2

This I Know

Some people enjoy a spiritual love life like the one that Elizabeth Payson Prentiss wrote about. As she considered her joyful experience with Jesus, Prentiss wrote: "To love Christ more is the deepest need, the constant cry of my soul. . . . Out in the woods and on my bed and out driving, when I am happy and busy, and when I am sad and idle, the whisper keeps going up for more love, more love, more love!"[1]

Then again, some people have a relationship with Christ that is not like that at all. They find it hard to love Jesus even a little bit, let alone love him more and more. In fact, they are not entirely sure what it looks like or feels like to love Jesus. And they are not entirely convinced that Jesus loves them, either. As one college student wrestled with heavy doubts about the Christian faith, his mother asked him whether he believed that Jesus loved him. The student's answer came after a long pause. "Minimally," he said.

What about you? Do you ever have your doubts about the love of God? Do you ever feel as if God loves you only minimally, if he loves you at all?

The Bible says that we love God because he first loved us (1 John 4:19). As we have seen, it also tells us that the Holy Spirit is the source of God's love in the life of the believer. But if we are not entirely sure that Jesus *does* love us, then how can we possibly love him? There is a deep and direct connection between loving and being loved. So in order for us to have more love for Jesus, we need to know more of his love for us. And when we have our doubts, it is desperately important for us to fight for the assurance of God's affection.

Doubting Your Doubts

Some of my favorite comments about the relationship between faith and doubt use insects as a basis for comparison, drawing connections between theology and entomology. Frederick Buechner takes a positive perspective when he writes, "Doubts are the ants in the pants of faith. They keep it awake and moving."[2] But the poet Roger White finds his spiritual doubts to be more of a nuisance: "A mosquito buzzes round my faith," he says—the mosquito of spiritual doubt.[3]

Many of us can identify with the poet's description. In our solitary moments the nagging questions whine away at our souls like so many mosquitoes. Is the Bible really true? Does God actually hear my prayers? Can I genuinely be forgiven? Will I definitely go to heaven when I die? Is there truly a God at all?

The novelist John Updike describes a Presbyterian minister who answers the last question in the negative. Under the influence of liberal scholarship, the man has serious questions about central doctrines of the Christian faith, until one day he gives in to his doubts and abandons his Christianity. As Updike tells it,

> The Reverend Clarence Arthur Wilmot, down in the rectory of the Fourth Presbyterian Church at the corner of Straight Street and Broadway, felt the last particles of his faith leave him. The sensation was distinct— a visceral surrender, a set of dark sparkling bubbles escaping upward. . . . His thoughts had slipped with quicksilver momentum into the recognition, which he had long withstood, that . . . there is no . . . God, nor should there be.
>
> Clarence's mind was like a many-legged, wingless insect [!] that had long and tediously been struggling to climb up the walls of a slick-walled porcelain basin; and now a sudden impatient wash of water swept it down into the drain. *There is no God*.[4]

Doubt can be a stimulus to faith, or an ongoing annoyance in the Christian life, or a fatal blow to someone's loose commitment to Jesus. It all depends on what we do with our doubts. So we should choose our insect wisely!

One thing we should always do with our doubts is to be honest about the fact that we have them. Doubt is *a struggle to be acknowledged*. Indeed, having doubts is a normal part of Christian experience. We see this repeatedly in the Scriptures. We see it in the story of Job, whose afflictions tempted him to doubt the goodness of the sovereignty of God. We see it in the life of Asaph, who looked around at the atheists he knew, saw what a good time they seemed to be having, and suddenly doubted whether God was worth it (Ps. 73:1–15). We see it in David, whose psalms testify to all the struggles of a doubting soul. We also see it in the desperate father who hoped that Jesus would heal his son from an evil spirit. "I do believe," he said to Jesus, but "help me overcome my unbelief" (Mark 9:24 NIV).

All of these believers were also doubters, sometimes. In a way, we even see this in Jesus himself, in his words from the cross, when he gathered up all of our darkest doubts and expressed them in the interrogative mood: "My God, my God, why have you forsaken me?" (Mark 15:34; cf. Ps. 22:1). Doubt is a struggle to be acknowledged—an ordinary dimension of spiritual experience for God's faithful people in a fallen world.

But doubt is also *a temptation to be resisted*. The main person who wants us to disbelieve is the Devil, which is why dealing with doubt can be such a dark struggle. The contested ground between faith and unbelief is a spiritual battlefield, and like any form of warfare, it calls for armed resistance.

Some believers spend too much time doubting their faith, and not enough time doubting their doubts. Yes, there are some reasonable questions that thoughtful people have always raised about the Christian faith. But there are also some very good questions that faithful people should raise about their spiritual doubts:

Have I studied what God has to say on this question, or have I been listening mainly to his detractors?

Am I well aware of how this doubt has been addressed in the history of Christian theology, or has my thinking been relatively superficial?

Have I been compromising with sin in ways that make it harder for me to hear God's voice and diminish my desire for the purity of his truth?

Is this a doubt that I have offered sincerely to God in prayer, or am I waiting to see if God measures up to my standards before I ask for his help?

All of the doubting believers that I mentioned earlier knew how to fight for the assurance of their faith. When Asaph had his doubts, he went to the temple and worshiped God anyway. Once he was there, he perceived, correctly, that turning away from God would only end in destruction (Ps. 73:16–28). When David had his doubts, he talked them over with God in prayer. And when the half-believing, half-doubting father in the Gospel of Mark wondered if his son would ever be delivered, he went to Jesus and prayed for the gift of triumphant faith.

These are all God-honoring ways to deal with spiritual doubts. Even doubting is something we can do to the glory of God, as long as we do it with God, and not against him. So as you seek the assurance of God's love, be sure to doubt your doubts!

Going Back to the Gospel of Love

Most of all, the assurance of God's love will come by going back to the gospel and listening again to the good news about Jesus Christ. If the gospel is what we are having trouble believing, then it may be tempting to ignore it. Instead, we ought to go back to the lowly manger and not stop until we have gone on to the bloody cross, the empty tomb, and the glorious throne of God, where Jesus reigns as the King of all kings.

When we go back to the story of Jesus like this and see him again in his gospel, we know that we are loved. We know this because everything Jesus has ever done for our salvation is a demonstration of his affection. The apostle Paul said it like this, in his letter to Titus: "When the goodness and loving kindness of God our Savior appeared, he saved us" (Titus 3:4–5). As soon as Jesus is introduced into the situation, love is there, and because love is there, we are saved.

In offering this assurance, the apostle Paul knows that

there is a darker side to life. The language he uses to describe what life is like without Christ, or before Christ, is dark and depressing. We were "foolish," he says, "led astray, slaves to various passions and pleasures, passing our days in malice and envy, hated by others and hating one another" (Titus 3:3).

This is what life is like without Christ, which explains why times of spiritual doubt can be so discouraging. The more trouble we have seeing Jesus, the more we wander into foolish thinking. The consequences are devastating: sinful patterns of self indulgence, angry conflicts with other people, and bitter thoughts about ourselves as well as others. If these are some of the struggles that we have— habitual sin, broken relationships, self-loathing—then we must not be seeing the love of Jesus the way that God wants us to see it.

Everything is different when we really do see Jesus. Titus 3:4 marks a turn in thought and a change in our destiny: "But when the goodness and loving kindness of God our Savior appeared, he saved us, not because of works done by us in righteousness, but according to his own mercy" (Titus 3:4–5).

What makes the transition from "before" to "after" is nothing that we can do for ourselves, but only what God can do for us. So the apostle proceeds to describe the loving way that God saves us: "by the washing of regeneration and renewal of the Holy Spirit, whom he poured out on us richly through Jesus Christ our Savior, so that being justi-

35

fied by his grace we might become heirs according to the hope of eternal life" (Titus 3:5–7). Many great doctrines of salvation are gathered together in these verses: regeneration, justification, sanctification, and glorification.

The Trinity is here, too. The way that God washes us clean, and gives us the gift of new spiritual birth, and declares us righteous, and makes us holy, and raises us up to glory, and gives us the hope of eternal life is by the love of God the Father, the grace of Jesus the Son, and the power of the Holy Spirit.

When He Appeared

Notice specifically what brings the change from hatred to love, from being lost to being saved: it is the loving-kindness of God in the appearance of his Son Jesus Christ. When he says that love "appeared," Paul is referring to the first advent of Jesus Christ—his coming into the world at his nativity—plus everything else that he proceeded to do for us through his life, ministry, death, resurrection, and ascension to glory.

The New Testament vocabulary related to *appearing* (Gk. *epiphaneia*) typically if not exclusively pertains to the coming of Christ as Savior.[5] Paul clearly uses the word that way back in Titus 2, where he says that "the grace of God appeared, bringing salvation for all people" (Titus 2:11). Another example occurs in the opening chapter of 2 Timothy, where Paul writes of the grace "which now has been manifested through the appearing of our Savior Christ Jesus, who abolished death and brought life and immortality to light through the gospel" (2 Tim. 1:10). The coming of Christ is the appearing of God's saving love.

What stunning joy Jesus brought to the people of God when he first appeared. We sing about this in some of our favorite Christmas carols: "Veiled in flesh the Godhead see; hail the incarnate Deity!" "Word of the Father, late in flesh appearing." "See, amid the winter's snow, born for us on earth below / see the tender Lamb appears, promised from eternal years."[6]

The love of God has appeared to us. It has come to us. It has entered our world, and as we open our arms to embrace it, this love is guaranteed to fill our minds and hearts. The appearance of Jesus is the entrance of our Father's love.

So when we find ourselves uncertain about the love of God—notice that I say "when," not "if"—one of the first places we should go is to the manger. There we see that love has come down to us from heaven. We are reminded that Jesus loved us enough to leave behind the glory of his holy throne and enter the misery of this fallen world. He is not far away from our suffering, but has entered in. He has done this because he loves us.

But of course Jesus did not stop there. Not merely his incarnation, but also his entire life was a demonstration of his affection. He loved by serving. He loved by teaching. He loved by healing and forgiving. Most of all, he loved us by dying on the cross for our sins. The crucifixion is the demonstration of our Savior's affection and the proof of our Father's love: "God shows his love for us in that while we were still sinners, Christ died for us" (Rom. 5:8; cf. John 3:16). Paul took this general truth and made it personal: "I live by faith in the Son of God, who loved me and gave himself for me" (Gal. 2:20). Why would a sinless man suffer the wrath and curse of holy judgment, dying a death for others that they deserved to die? Only for love. Indeed, "greater love has no one than this, that someone lay down his life for his friends" (John 15:13; cf. 1 John 3:16).

The love of Jesus does not stop even there, with his death. On the third day the Father raised his Son from the grave, by the power of the Holy Spirit, and this too was a gift of God's love. Scripture says it was "because of the great love with which he loved us" that "even when we were dead in our trespasses" God "made us alive together with Christ" and "raised us up with him" (Eph. 2:4–6). The whole drama of our salvation is a love story from start to finish—the love that has appeared to us in Jesus Christ. Truly, it is a love that will never end, because nothing in time or eternity can ever separate us from the love that God has for us in Jesus Christ (Rom. 8:35–39). When the brilliant nineteenth-century scientist Michael Faraday was on his deathbed, someone asked, "Sir, what are your speculations now?" Faraday replied, "Speculation? I have none, thank God. I am not resting my dying soul on guess-work, but on the finished work of Jesus Christ. 'I know whom

I have believed and am persuaded that He is able to keep that which I have committed to Him against that Day.'"[7]

Do you know that God loves you—not minimally, but maximally? Do you believe that Jesus has appeared for you as much as for anyone? If you are having your doubts, then let him tell you how much he loves you again in the gospel story of your salvation.

More Love for Jesus

Having a deeper assurance of God's saving love in Jesus Christ changes everything. Here is how one young alumnus described the spiritual transformation that took place in his life during his last year of college, as he pursued the gospel with a group of Christian men:

> I began to encounter the living Christ as never before. God had revealed Himself to be "the God who is there" in the past, yet it seemed as though He had never revealed what He was like, who He was. At least, He did not do so to the extent that He did during that year. During those months, I saw more of my own depravity, my own tendency towards wickedness, and my stubborn hardness of heart than I could dare handle, yet simultaneously, I began to see the truth of the Gospel of Jesus Christ to be more glorious and wonderful than I ever dared to dream.
>
> The fact that Christ associates Himself with sinners, rebellious and hostile, and loves them was a

truth that began to melt my heart. He really loves sinners. And He doesn't love through gritted teeth or with mixed ulterior motives. He loves with sincerity. It is a strong love. A deep love. Yet, it is a love that does not simply pass over sin, excusing it as insignificant.

Oh, to the contrary, He, Jesus Christ, the Son of God, did for us what we could never do for ourselves. He lived a perfect and holy life in complete submission to the Father's will. He died a willing, God-ordained, sacrificial, substitutionary, wrath-absorbing death on behalf of sinners. And he was raised, thus defeating death and showing that God the Father had accepted Christ's sacrifice. . . . This is GREAT NEWS that must be dwelled upon by believers.[8]

As we dwell on the great news of Jesus, his saving death, and his glorious resurrection, our hearts will grow more in love with him. His deep, strong love will triumph over sin and hatred, enabling us to become the lovers that God has designed us to become.

This chapter began with a quote from Elizabeth Payson Prentiss, who described more love for Christ as the "deepest need" and "constant cry" of her soul. Prentiss expressed this desire most clearly and most famously in the words of her best-known hymn:

More love to thee, O Christ, more love to thee!
Hear thou the prayer I make on bended knee;

This is my earnest plea, more love, O Christ, to thee,
More love to thee, more love to thee!

The words of this prayer take on added significance in the context of the hymn-writer's biography. Prentiss suffered the sad loss of two of her three children, who died just a few weeks apart. As a grieving mother she was inconsolable, almost despairing of life itself. These are the words she used to describe the agony of that loss: "Empty hands, a worn-out, exhausted body, and unutterable longings to flee from a world that has so many sharp experiences."[9]

Yet Elizabeth Payson Prentiss had the faith to doubt her doubts. She continued to listen to the gospel of Jesus, and this brought her through her doubtful sufferings to a place of assurance in God's love. And this assurance came, in turn, with a deep desire to offer Jesus her loving heart. In one of her poems, Prentiss reflected on her earthly sorrows and wrote: "One child and two green graves are mine / This is God's gift to me." Her loss was great, but her words were not bitter, because she went on to say this: "A bleeding, fainting, broken heart / This is my gift to Thee."[10]

What gift will you offer to God? As you consider his great love for you in Jesus, give him more of your loving heart.

3

With All We Have

One summer I received a letter that was critical of Wheaton College in general and its president in particular. This is not uncommon; like most leaders, I hear a fair number of complaints. However, this particular letter ended in a way that brought me up short. My correspondent said, "Instead of sitting at your computer writing some book about love, you should get out of your office and actually start loving people," or words to that effect.

After I read the letter I had to laugh, because it was so true. The woman who wrote the letter didn't even know me, although she must have seen my little book *Loving the Way Jesus Loves*. Nevertheless, it seemed as if she had been sitting in the corner of my office and then following me around the rest of the day. I say this because she was absolutely right: I'm a lot better at knowing what to do than doing it, and a lot better at telling people what the Bible says about love than actually loving.

As I explained in the preface to this book, I need more love for Jesus. Maybe you do, too. Maybe you know about Jesus without really knowing Jesus—not in a loving way. Maybe you used to love Jesus more than you do now. Or maybe you are not even sure what it means to love Jesus. In all honesty, he is more like an acquaintance than a lover. Although one time you asked him to be your Savior, and sometimes you sing his praises, it is rare for you to speak to him directly and say, "Jesus, I love you."

If these words describe you at all, then maybe our journey into the heart of the Son of God will help. By the work of the Holy Spirit, who is the source of all true love, God can take something that the apostle Peter said and make it more and more true for us: "Though you have not seen him, you love him. Though you do not now see him, you believe in him and rejoice with joy that is inexpressible and filled with glory" (1 Pet. 1:8).

The First and Greatest Commandment

We find the command to love God—and to love him with everything we have—many places in Scripture. We find it first in the Law of Moses: "You shall love the LORD your God with all your heart and with all your soul and with all your might" (Deut. 6:5). The verse is so comprehensive that immediately we sense it expresses a whole way of life: a life of love.

Moses repeated this call again and again for the children of God: "And now, Israel, what does the LORD your God require of you, but to fear the LORD your God, to walk in all his ways, to love him, to serve the LORD your God with all your heart and with all your soul" (Deut. 10:12; cf. 11:13; 13:3; 30:6). We find the same thing in the commands of Joshua (Josh. 22:5) and the prayers of Solomon (1 Kings 8:23; 2 Chron. 6:14). It is one of the most basic commands in the Old Testament: love God.

It is not surprising, then, that we find the same statement repeated by Jesus Christ, who explicitly added the command to love God with all our *minds*. When a lawyer asked him to identify the greatest commandment of God, Jesus responded by saying, "You shall love the Lord your God with all your heart and with all your soul and with all your mind" (Matt. 22:37). Mark and Luke give slightly different forms of this saying by adding the word "strength" (Mark 12:30; Luke 10:27). The call of the new covenant is the same as the old: in loving God, we give him our "all."

Members of Wheaton College make the same commitment at the beginning of the Community Covenant we sign. Sometimes people make the mistake of focusing on what that document is against, the places where we say "no" for the good of our campus community and the glory of God. But the Community Covenant mainly says "yes," starting with the first and greatest of all commandments. We are called, the document says, to "love God with our whole being, including our minds."

We should be careful to take this requirement the right

way. When the Bible tells us to love God with mind, heart, soul, and strength, it is not telling us to do four different things but giving us four different ways to do one and the same thing. Moses was not trying to make a careful distinction between heart and soul, and when Jesus added the word "mind," he was not giving a new commandment. The point is to love God with everything we have. This is driven home by almost poetic repetition. In adding "all your mind" and "all your strength" to "all your heart" and "all your soul," Jesus makes the strongest possible claim on our affections.

Loving Jesus "with all your mind" is not something different than loving him with heart and strength; it really amounts to the same thing. Still, it is appropriate to take this command and apply it to the life of the mind. Later in this book we will consider what it means to love God with all our hearts. After all, there is an emotional dimension to our affections. But there is also an intellectual dimension. Indeed, A. W. Tozer wondered "whether there is on earth, anything that is as exquisitely lovely as a brilliant mind that is aglow with the love of God."[1] So first we consider what it means to love God with all our minds.

The Affectionate Intellect

The mind is a good place to begin, as I tried to explain to my brother-in-law one time when we were talking about family mottoes. He pointed out that some families have a motto that reflects their history or expresses their character. I said that if I had to give a motto for my family growing up it would be: "Love the Lord your God with all your mind."

My brother-in-law waited for me to say something more, because of course there is more to the verse. When he realized that I was finished, he burst out laughing. "That's *all*?" he said. "What about the rest of the verse— you know, loving God with all your heart and all your strength?"

"Well, we believe in that, too," I said, somewhat defensively, "but you have to focus on something. Besides," I added, "loving God with all your mind is a good place to start."

And so it is. What we think has a strong influence on what we feel. John Piper explains the connection like this: "Right thinking about God exists to serve right feelings for God."[2]

If this is true, then loving Jesus with all our minds will help us love him in other ways, too. But how do we actually *do* that? What are some good ways to love Jesus with our minds as part of loving him with all we have?

The simplest and maybe the most important way is to use our minds to meditate on the words that Jesus speaks to us in Holy Scripture. In his book *Discovering Lectio Divina*, Jim Wilhoit describes the devotional reading of Scripture as "the reading of a lover"—"the relaxed waiting that is as attentive to the relationship as it is to the text."[3]

If we ever wonder why we do not seem to love Jesus very much—at least not as much as we should—maybe this is one of the reasons why: we are not reading the Bible in one of the ways we should. We are reading it in worship services, perhaps, or reading it for a class or study group. We are reading the Bible for content and maybe for application, but not for a relationship.

If we want to love Jesus with all we have, we should read his Word the way a lover would, as a message from our beloved. Whenever we open our Bibles, we should pray, "Lord Jesus, I am not just here for these words; I am here for you, and for the love message you want to send from your heart to mine." God has promised to meet us in his Word, which makes Bible-reading a place to rendezvous with our Savior. "So willing is he," wrote Søren Kierkegaard about the infinitely loving God, "to become involved with a person that he has written love letters to us in his word, has proposed to us and said: come, come."[4] When we respond to this invitation, we are loving God with all our minds.

Another way to love Jesus with all we have is to value his handiwork in the world around us. Christians in the academy do this in their course work and scholarship. We explore the wonders of the natural world, or work with sight and sound—not only through art and music, but also through the auditory gift of the spoken word. But we do not have to be in a classroom, a laboratory, or a studio to do this. All we have to do is walk across the lawn and notice the green leaf turning to gold or watch the red hawk perched on the woody branch. By attending to creation with a heart of praise, we engage our minds lovingly toward our Creator. We love Jesus by taking delight in the power and beauty he has displayed in the world all around us. "If I love the Lover," wrote Francis Schaeffer, "I love what the Lover has made."[5]

In her own simple way, Rose Binney Salter understood this principle well. Rose was an African slave who worshiped in Jonathan Edwards's congregation in Stockbridge, Massachusetts. Another minister once spoke with her about how she came to faith in Jesus Christ. By way of reply, Rose recounted her experience of conversion:

> Den I come in, take my pail, and go out milk my cow. Just when I sat down, and lean my pail forward, to milk my cow, sun rise and shine right into my pail. I look! I don't know what's matter. Well, I nebber did see sun shine so all my life! Den I look at clouds: dey look just so, too! Den I look at trees, dey all look just so too.[6]

The minister was unclear as to what Rose meant, exactly, so he interrupted her to ask, "You say you never saw the sun shine so: you never saw the clouds look so; and you never saw the trees look so. I wish you to tell me how they appeared; and what it was you saw in them." All that Rose could say in response was, "O I don't know, Sir; *only all full of God, ebry where!*"[7] When a mind is in love with

49

Jesus, this is what it sees: a world full of the wonders he has made.

We love Jesus with all we have when we offer him the very best of our thinking. A mind that truly loves Jesus is not content with quick or easy answers, but thinks an issue all the way through. It does not simply collect a set of mental prejudices, which are then reinforced by reading and listening to sources that share the same perspective, but it thoughtfully considers countervailing opinions. Then it weighs and ponders and ultimately discovers the real truth about something. Using our minds wisely and comprehensively is a way to honor our Maker.

In doing this, the affectionate intellect never leaves Jesus out, but always includes him in the thought process. This is only natural, because when we are in love, we think about our beloved all the time. We do what John Calvin Webster talked about in a dedicatory address to the faculty and students of Wheaton College in 1868. The renowned scholar of logic and rhetoric said, "I take it to be the grand purpose of this college, not merely to bring out, strengthen, and refine, but to sanctify the powers of the mind—to subsidize all human learning to the precepts and instructions of the Great Teacher."[8] Our thinking is not autonomous; it is lovingly surrendered to the lordship of Jesus Christ. Whether we happen to be thinking about biology, philosophy, anthropology, or any of the other liberal arts and sciences, we always keep him in mind.

With All *His* Mind

There are many good reasons to love God with all we have. For one thing, Jesus made it very clear that this is the First and Greatest Commandment that God ever gave us. Furthermore, loving our Savior with all our minds will help us love him in other ways, too. Here is how Thomas Vincent explained the influence that love for Christ has on the whole life of the Christian disciple:

> Christ knows the command and influence which love to Him, in the truth and strength of it, has; how it will engage all the other affections of His disciples for Him; that if He has their love, their desires will be chiefly after Him. Their delights will be chiefly in Him; their hopes and expectations will be chiefly from Him; . . . He knows that love will engage and employ for Him all the powers and faculties of their soul; their thoughts will be brought into captivity and obedience unto Him; their understandings will be employed in seeking and finding out His truths; . . . their wills will choose and refuse, according to His direction and revealed pleasure.
>
> All their senses and the members of their bodies will be His servants. Their eyes will see for Him, their ears will hear for Him, their tongues will speak for Him, their hands will work for Him, their feet will walk for Him. All their gifts and talents will be at His devotion and service. If He has their love, they will be ready to do for Him what He requires. They will

suffer for Him whatever He calls them to. If they have much love to Him, they will not think much of denying themselves, taking up His cross, and following Him wherever He leads them.[9]

Loving God will also help us to love one another. The more full we are with love for Jesus, the more his love will spill over into other relationships.

These are all good reasons to love Jesus with all our minds. But perhaps the greatest motivation for responding to Jesus with an affectionate intellect is this: we should love Jesus with all of our minds because he loves us with all of *his* mind.

Our deepest motivations for following Jesus always come from the outside, not the inside. We do not begin with what we do for him, but with what he has done for us. Everything in the Christian life flows from the grace that God has for us in Jesus Christ. So if we are looking for the motivation to love Jesus with all our minds, we should begin with the fact that he loves us with all of his mind—he always has, and he always will.

"In the beginning was the Word," John says at the opening of his Gospel, using the term *Word* to introduce the mysteries of the mind of the Son of God. Jesus Christ is "the Word." He is the living person with the rational principle at the heart of the universe. John proceeds to tell us that the mind of Christ was in the beginning, making all things. Nothing was ever made except through the Word, which means that the whole creation is a revelation of the mind of Jesus Christ.

Every now and then I encounter a fact about the natural world that blows my mind, and I am reminded again that the universe was designed by an infinite intelligence. I had this experience when I read *The Immortal Life of Henrietta Lacks* and learned that five thousand cells can fit on the head of a pin.[10] Amazing! There is a world of wonder that is invisible to the naked eye.

Several nights after encountering this fact, I woke my two little girls at midnight so we could go out and watch the Perseid meteor showers. Every August, as the earth passes through the trail of debris along the orbit of the comet Swift-Tuttle, our atmosphere is pierced by flaming meteors that appear to stream from the constellation Perseus. On a black and moonless night in northern Wisconsin, we went out on the dock, laid on our backs, and counted the "shooting stars." The next morning I asked Karoline, age seven, if she enjoyed the meteor shower. "Yeah," she said, "but it was kind of scary."

I knew what she meant. Under the vast canopy of space, we are as small as one of the five thousand cells that fit on the head of a pin. When we have these spine-tingling experiences, we know that we are having a direct encounter with the mind of our Maker. Whether we peer into a microscope or look through a telescope, everything we see has been designed by Jesus Christ.

But there is more, because the same mind that made us

also came up with the plan to save us. Consider the story that Whittaker Chambers told about his spiritual awakening. Although he later became famous for his testimony against Americans who spied for the Soviet Union, at the time Chambers was a Communist himself—a devout believer in the materialist philosophy of Marx and Lenin. In his autobiography, he describes the change that happened to him one day when he was feeding his daughter breakfast:

> My daughter was in her high chair. I was watching her eat. She was the most miraculous thing that had ever happened in my life. I liked to watch her even when she smeared porridge on her face or dropped it meditatively on the floor. My eye came to rest on the delicate convolutions of her ear—those intricate, perfect ears. The thought passed through my mind: "No, those ears were not created by any chance coming together of atoms in nature. They could have been created only by immense design."

Although Chambers was not yet ready to admit it, such design presupposed the existence of a Designer. So that was the day, he later testified, when "the finger of God was first laid upon my forehead."[11]

Eventually Chambers came to faith in Jesus Christ and saw the mind of God at work in the plan of redemption, which is a demonstration of divine love from beginning to end. To begin at the beginning, the Bible says explicitly that we were predestined "in love" to be adopted as the children of God (Eph. 1:4–5). When the Father, the Son, and the Holy Spirit put their mind together to map out the plan of salvation, they did it with love for all their sons and daughters. And when the Son came into the world to work the plan, he set his mind on doing what the Father called him to do: preach the gospel, perform the miracles of the kingdom, and live with perfect obedience to the law of God—one mind totally surrendered to the purposes of God, with the goal of our salvation.

Then came the night before the crucifixion, when Jesus endured the mental anguish of Gethsemane, wondering if there was any other way to save us. But as he reasoned with the Father, he knew that there was no other way. Only a perfect sacrifice, paid in blood, would atone for sin. This had been worked out in the mind of God before the beginning of time. And there, in Gethsemane, God the Son thought it through again: God could only be just and the justifier of the ungodly through the cross (Rom. 4:15). So Jesus went down from Gethsemane and up to Calvary. This was the choice of his reason and the demonstration of his love.

Understand that Jesus loved you with all his mind all the way to the cross. And even as he surrendered his mind to death, he was reasoning forward to the resurrection, believing that his Father would raise him up again by the power of the Holy Spirit.

A Relationship with a Future

This is what motivates us to love Jesus with all of our minds: he has loved us with all of his mind. "How precious to me are your thoughts, O God!" wrote the psalmist. "How vast is the sum of them! If I would count them, they are more than the sand" (Ps. 139:17–18).

When I consider everything that Jesus has done for me—the way his infinite, affectionate intellect has been at work in my creation and redemption—I want to love Jesus more. What about you?

Soon we will see Jesus face to face. Whether it happens when we die and enter his glory, or whether we become eyewitnesses to the second coming, the day will come when our Savior takes us into his arms. When that day comes, I want to know Jesus—really know him—because I have grown to love him.

An example of this kind of love—love that anticipates an immediate encounter with the Son of God—comes from a conversation that Dame Cicely Saunders once had with a patient named Louie. Dr. Saunders is widely recognized as the founder of the hospice care movement, and as a devout Christian, she was keenly interested in the spiritual lives of her patients. Louie suffered from a painful bone condition that kept her confined to bed. As the two women spoke about Louie's prolonged sufferings, Dr. Saunders sought to encourage her friend by looking forward to her life after death, and specifically to the moment when she would meet Jesus face to face. "And when it has really happened," she asked, "what's the first thing that you will say to him?" Louie answered immediately: "Oh! I'll say, 'I know you.'"[12]

Every true lover of Christ can give the same testimony. Our relationship with him is just beginning—a love relationship that will never end.

4

What Makes Love Extravagant

Late one night, on a dark and secluded highway near Charlotte, North Carolina, NFL wide receiver Rae Carruth and his accomplices brutally murdered his girlfriend Cherica. Remarkably—almost miraculously—the child that Cherica was carrying in her womb survived: Chancellor Lee Adams. More remarkable still is the testimony of Chancellor's grandmother Saundra, and her resolute commitment to forgiveness.

Chancellor was born with severe brain damage—the result of all the blood his mother lost between the highway where she was shot and the hospital where she died. Today his grandmother bears the tender burden of clothing, feeding, and cleaning up a growing teenager who cannot care for himself. Yet far from feeling sorry for herself, or getting angry with her daughter's killer, she perseveres in the grace of forgiveness.

When Carruth was sentenced for his crime, Saundra Adams was invited to testify. After describing her daily struggle to care for a man-child with cerebral palsy, she spoke these words to the judge: "Rae Carruth has not shown one single ounce of remorse, to me or anyone in my family, there's not been one 'I'm sorry about what happened to your daughter.' But in my heart, because I'm a Christian, as an act of my will, and because I know it's out of obedience to God, I am *forgiving* Rae Carruth."[1]

The journalist who recounted Saundra's story in the pages of *Sports Illustrated* marveled at her extravagant love and rare forgiveness. But the basis for that love is not hard to find. Before she forgave anyone else, Saundra Adams experienced forgiveness herself, through the cross where Jesus died for her sins. Her life of extravagant love is the grateful response of a sinner who has found true forgiveness in Jesus Christ.

The Extravagance of a Sinner's Love

Perhaps nowhere do we see the connection between loving and being forgiven more clearly than in the story Luke told about a woman who anointed Jesus's feet with sorry tears and sweet perfume. Luke highlights the extravagance of her love by contrasting it with the scornful contempt of a self-righteous man. The contrast helps us to see ourselves in one of these two people, and in the way they responded to Jesus. Who am I: the person who loves or the person who condemns?

Strangely enough, this incident occurred at a Pharisee's house, where Jesus had been invited for dinner. While people were eating, something surprising happened—something so surprising that Luke introduces it with an exclamation: "And *behold*, a woman of the city, who was a sinner, when she learned that he was reclining at table in the Pharisee's house, brought an alabaster flask of ointment, and standing behind him at his feet, weeping, she began to wet his feet with her tears and wiped them with the hair of her head and kissed his feet and anointed them with the ointment" (Luke 7:37–38).

To understand this beautiful gesture, it helps to know something about dinner parties in biblical times. Large homes had an open floor plan in those days, and typically a wealthy man like this Pharisee would host his guests in the courtyard. The meal would have been a semipublic occasion—more like a block party than a private dinner. Even people who were not invited might stop by for a chat, and perhaps sit around the edge of the courtyard.

It *was* uncommon for a woman like this to show up at a house like this and do what she did for Jesus. We do not know her name. In fact, virtually the only thing we know about her is that she was a sinner. This is mentioned three times: by Luke, by the Pharisee, and by Jesus himself (Luke 7:37, 39, 47). Some people assume that she was a prostitute, and they may be right: Luke describes her as someone off the streets of the city. It really doesn't matter, though, because a sinner's a sinner.

And this is why the woman came to see Jesus. Sinful as she was, she knew that Jesus was the friend of sinners. So when she heard that he was dining at the Pharisee's house, she went to him with her perfume, hoping to worship at his feet. When she arrived, there he was. Presumably, he was reclining in the ancient style, with his legs stretched behind him and his feet away from the table.

At first the woman simply stood there, looking at Jesus with adoring eyes, not daring to touch him. But soon she was overcome with emotion. Maybe she told herself not to cry, but if she did, she couldn't help it. Here was the lover of her soul and the friend of her sinner's heart. As she thought about all the wrong things that she had done, somehow she knew that Jesus had mercy for her. Then the tears started to flow—tears of relief, gratitude, and joy.

I told this story to my son when he was two years old, and it was hard for him to understand why the woman was crying. "Why tears, Daddy?" he asked. The answer is that she was overwhelmed by the grace that God was offering to her in Jesus. She was weeping with the gratitude of sin forgiven.

As the woman looked down, suddenly she realized that her Savior's feet were wet with her tears. Almost without thinking, perhaps, she began to wipe them with her hair. It was bad enough for a woman with her reputation to show up at a Pharisee's house uninvited; in those days some people also considered it inappropriate for a woman to let down her hair in public. But this woman no longer cared what other people thought. She was so in love with Jesus that she forgot herself completely. Passionately, but not erotically, she let her hair fall on his feet.

Nor did the sinful, grateful woman stop there. She proceeded to pour out her perfume, anointing her Savior's feet with scented oil. This was an expensive gift, almost certainly the most precious thing she owned, but she poured it all on the feet of Jesus. *He* was the treasure of her soul.

This was a demonstration of astonishing affection. When the woman poured out her perfume, she was pouring out her heart with the fragrance of her love. Then she kissed Jesus's feet, and if the tense of the verb is any indication, she went on kissing them. Truly, this is one of the most beautiful things that anyone has ever done for Jesus. The entire scene portrays the extravagant love of a forgiven sinner

I wonder: how would you respond, if you could stand before Jesus at this very moment? Would you fall into his arms? Would you bow at his feet in worship? Would you weep with uncontrollable joy that all your sins are totally forgiven and completely forgotten?

The Scorn of a Hypocrite's Contempt

The Pharisee did none of these things. Frankly, he was offended by what the woman was doing and embarrassed by what he considered to be an awkward display of unrestrained emotion. Luke writes: "Now when the Pharisee who had invited him saw this, he said to himself, 'If this man were a prophet, he would have known who and what sort of woman this is who is touching him, for she is a sinner'" (Luke 7:39).

Spoken like a true Pharisee! The man was quick to condemn other people for their sins, and when he did, he placed himself in a different category. *He* was righteous, but *they* were sinners. Such judgmentalism was typical of the Pharisees we meet in the Gospels. With their holier-than-thou attitude, the Pharisees were always looking down on other people, snorting with indignation over their sins. Yet they themselves were as guilty as anyone.

Notice the contempt in the Pharisee's words. Not only did he call the woman "a sinner," but he also alluded to "what sort of woman" she was. This was highly pejorative and probably had sexual overtones.

The Pharisee had nearly as much disdain for Jesus. Until now he had wondered whether Jesus might be a prophet. Now he was sure that Jesus wasn't a prophet, because holy men do not associate with sinners. Or at least this is what the Pharisee thought. As far as he was concerned, God was for good people, not for bad people. So a righteous man would avoid having any contact with sinners. If Jesus were a real prophet, he would have known better.

By thinking this way, the Pharisee thought that he was maintaining high moral standards, but in fact he was graceless, merciless, and loveless. Kent Hughes describes him as a man with "an arctic heart, a permafrost of the soul."[2] All the Pharisee could do with sinners was to condemn them; he had no grace to give.

To help us see ourselves in this story, Luke deliberately shows us two completely different responses to Jesus, based on two totally different attitudes about sin and grace. There were many contrasts between these two people. One had a high social position, and the other was an outcast. One was a host, and the other wasn't even a guest. One was angry; the other was overwhelmed with joy. One was still evaluating Jesus, while the other had decided to trust him with her entire life. But the fundamental contrast was this: only one of these people believed that God had grace for sinners. Even without saying a word, the woman proved by her actions that she trusted Jesus for the forgiveness of her sins. She believed in his grace. But the Pharisee did not have room for grace in his theology at all. He believed that grace was unavailable to sinners like that woman and unnecessary for a righteous person like himself.

From a spiritual standpoint, it is easy to see which of these two people was more attractive, and which of them had the right response to Jesus. But the important question for us to ask is, which of the two sinners is more like us? What comes more naturally: rejoicing with amazement that someone like you could ever be forgiven, or coldly judging that some people do not deserve to be forgiven? Are you more of a lover, or a condemner?

One of the best ways to test our grasp of God's grace is to see how we respond to the people we think of as "sinners." What do we say about them? How do we treat them? What are we doing to reach out to them with the love of Jesus? Sadly, many Christians do not care enough to get involved in the lives of people in spiritual trouble. They do not touch "sinners," and they do not let "sinners" touch them.

Our calling as Christians is to share the love of Christ with people who need his grace. In the same way that Jesus came to seek and to save the lost, and in the same way that he has touched our own lives with mercy, we are called to reach out with his love.

How do you respond to the girl who has a reputation for sleeping around, the homeless man who acts like a drug addict, the gay couple in your apartment building, the family member who criticizes you for believing the gospel, the pastor whose life fails to measure up to his doctrine, or the racist who is blind to his bigotry? How strong are the relationships you are building with the obvious sinners in your life? Often, we do not have relationships with them at all, or if we do, our contempt for them shows through. They can tell what we really think of them, and this may prevent them from ever wanting to hear what we want to tell them about Jesus.

But what would happen if we really believed that God has grace for sinners—not just for us, but for everyone? What would happen if we embraced lost and difficult people instead of avoiding them? What would happen in their lives, and what would happen in our lives? The way for us to make the difference in the world that God is calling us to make is to believe that he has grace for sinners.

What Makes the Difference

This true story from the life of Jesus does something more than merely show the contrast between two kinds of people; it also tells us what makes the difference.

As the Pharisee sat muttering to himself and thinking unkind thoughts, he was about to find out that Jesus really *was* a prophet. Not only did Jesus know what kind of woman was washing his feet, but he also knew what kind of man was sitting across from him at the table! So Jesus told a little story, which went like this: "A certain money-lender had two debtors. One owed five hundred denarii, and the other fifty. When they could not pay, he cancelled the debt of both. Now which of them will love him more?" (Luke 7:41–42).

The answer was obvious, but Simon was wary of a setup, so he answered cautiously: "The one, I suppose, for whom he cancelled the larger debt." The Pharisee was right, of course. Five hundred denarii was nearly two years' wages, and anyone forgiven so large a debt would be eternally grateful (v. 43).

Jesus was not talking about economics, however; he was talking about the great debt of our sin, and the grace that demands our gratitude. So he proceeded to apply his parable: "Turning toward the woman he said to Simon,

'Do you see this woman?'" (v. 44). In one sense the man *did* see the woman; he had been looking at her ever since she started touching Jesus. But in another sense he didn't see her at all—not the way God saw her. Simon could not see the woman that she was becoming through Christ and his forgiveness.

In asking Simon if he saw the woman, Jesus was trying to help the man see himself. Jesus said: "I entered your house; you gave me no water for my feet, but she has wet my feet with her tears and wiped them with her hair. You gave me no kiss, but from the time I came in she has not ceased to kiss my feet. You did not anoint my head with oil, but she has anointed my feet with ointment" (vv. 44–46). The Pharisee had done almost nothing for Jesus. He had not even fulfilled the basic duties of ordinary hospitality, which shows that he had nearly as much contempt for Jesus as he had for the sinful woman.

Sadly, there are times when we treat Jesus the same way. There was a time, maybe years ago, when we invited him into our hearts. But how much hospitality have we given him lately? Have we honored him in worship and greeted him with prayer, or have we been indifferent to his Spirit's presence in our lives? If so, then we are as guilty as Simon for treating the Son of God with shocking contempt.

By contrast, the sinful, grateful woman did everything she could for Jesus—everything Simon failed to do, and more. Rather than bringing water, she wet Jesus's feet with her tears. Instead of giving him a peck on the cheek, she kept on kissing and kissing him. She did not anoint his head, but his feet, and then wiped them with her long, beautiful hair.

What made the difference between these two people? To Jesus, the answer was obvious: the woman knew that she had been forgiven. So he laid out the logic of this to the Pharisee, "I tell you, her sins, which are many, are forgiven—for she loved much." Then he added words that should have pierced Simon's soul: "He who is forgiven little, loves little" (v. 47). Suddenly the meaning of the parable becomes clear. The more people have been forgiven, the more they love. The best lovers, therefore, are forgiven sinners.

We see this connection from the woman's love, which proved that the great debt of her sin had been forgiven. Everyone knew that she was a sinner, including the woman herself, and also Jesus, who did not overlook her transgressions. Nevertheless, she was fully forgiven, as the story tells us not once, or twice, but three times (vv. 47, 48, and 49). Yet the woman was no longer defined by her depravity. She had discovered that with Jesus there is enough forgiveness for all our sin, even if we are the biggest sinners in the world. All of this was proven by the woman's love. Jonathan Edwards rightly said, "All gracious affections that are a sweet aroma to Christ, and that fill the soul of a Christian with a heavenly sweetness and fragrancy, are brokenhearted affections. A truly Christian love, either to God or men is a humble broken-hearted love."[3]

But where did this leave Simon? What did his response reveal about the true condition of *his* heart? Well, the less people have been forgiven, the less they love, and since he loved so little, it is doubtful whether he had been forgiven at all. Maybe his sins seemed much smaller than the kinds of sins that the woman committed. Yet he was a debtor, too, and the real difference between them was not the size of their debt, but the fact that only one of them had asked to be forgiven. When Jesus said, "He who is forgiven little, loves little" (v. 47), obviously he was talking about Simon the Pharisee.

Once again, this story searches our hearts. Do we have an obvious and extravagant affection for Jesus, or do we place limits on how much we give of ourselves in worship or ministry? Do we see the full extent of our sin, or are we inclined to think that someone else is a bigger sinner than we are?

Some people are like Francis of Assisi, who famously said: "There is nowhere a more wretched and miserable sinner than I." Others are more like the wealthy duchess whom the Countess of Huntingdon invited to hear the famous evangelist George Whitefield. That proud woman was offended to receive the invitation; she had heard enough about Whitefield's preaching to know that she did not want anyone telling her that she needed to repent. Her precise words are recorded in the angry note that she sent back to the countess who invited her to hear the gospel: "It is monstrous to be told, that you have a heart as sinful as the common wretches that crawl on the earth. This is highly offensive and insulting; and I cannot but wonder that your Ladyship should relish any sentiments so much at variance with high rank and good breeding."[4]

The more we feel that we do not need to be forgiven, the more self-righteous we become. And the more self-righteous we become, the less love we have for Jesus, or anyone else. This is an area where we all need to examine ourselves: Am I doing the minimum, or am I pouring out my life like fragrant perfume? If we love Jesus little, it must be because we have little idea how much we have been forgiven.

It is only when we have a deep sense of our own personal sin against God that we fully grasp the wonder of his grace for us in Jesus Christ. Then we know how large a debt we have—the debt that was cancelled at Calvary. Then we know how many of our sins Christ had to pay for when he died on the cross. And then we know the great debt of love that we now owe to Jesus.

How to Respond

John Newton is perhaps most famous for writing "Amazing Grace," which is a hymn of gratitude for sins forgiven. But Newton did not find it any easier to love Jesus than most of us do. "So much forgiven, so little, little love," he wrote just a few weeks before composing his beloved hymn. "So many mercies, so few returns. Such great privileges, and a life so sadly below them."[5]

Sometimes we feel like John Newton: loveless toward our loving Savior. But Jesus wants our love for him to grow. The way to show him our love is not by kissing him, necessarily, or anointing him with perfume, or wiping his feet with our hair, but there are other ways. Tell Jesus that you are sorry for your many, many sins. Sing his praise with passion. Speak words of affection to him in prayer. Give away as much of yourself as you can. Then reach out to other sinners who need his grace, including people you are tempted to look down on, even people that no one else would touch.

This is the debt we owe for all the sins that God has forgiven: not just tears and perfume, but lives poured out for Jesus with extravagant love.

5

What Love Does

With some trepidation, Tevye the milkman tells his wife Golde that he has given their daughter Hodel permission to marry her tutor, Perchik. Golde objects, vociferously. "What??? He's poor! He has nothing, absolutely nothing!"

In response, Tevye observes that Hodel and Perchik are deeply in love. This puts him in a reflective mood, and as he considers his own marriage, Tevye asks Golde the question that is at the heart of their covenant relationship: "Do you love me?"

At first Golde can hardly understand the question. "Do I what?" she exclaims. Then she tries to dismiss Tevye: "With our daughters getting married / And this trouble in the town / You're upset, you're worn out / Go inside, go lie down!"

"Maybe it's indigestion," Golde mutters, half to herself, half to Tevye. But the man is persistent. He continues to press, forcing his wife to make a declaration. He wants to know if she really loves him. And as she looks back on twenty-five years of washing her husband's clothes, cooking his meals, cleaning his house, raising his children, and milking his cow, she reaches the inescapable conclusion that over the years she has learned to love the man she lives with. "If that's not love," she says, after a lifetime of service, "what is?"

This touching and humorous scene from *Fiddler on the Roof* contains a profoundly biblical insight: love is as love does. Love is not merely an affection of the heart or an attitude of the will; it is also the action of a person's life. True love comes to expression in practical, often sacrificial deeds of service.

If You Love Me

Once we understand how active love is, we can find thousands of ways to love Jesus more, which is the goal of this book. We began by learning that love for Jesus is not something we work up on our own (which is impossible anyway), but something God works into us by the Spirit. We observed that although doubt is a normal part of the Christian life, fighting for the assurance of our faith grounds us more deeply in the love of God. We considered the First and Greatest Commandment, which is to love God with everything we have, including our intellect. What motivates us to love the Lord our God "with all our mind" is knowing that Jesus loves us with all of *his* mind.

And we have seen that the more we are forgiven—like the woman who anointed the feet of Jesus with sorry tears and sweet perfume—the more extravagant our love will be.

But how do we *show* our love? What are some practical ways to love Jesus more? One of the best places to turn for an answer is to the words of Jesus himself, who said that every one of his commandments is another opportunity to love him.

We learn this from something that Jesus said on the night that he was betrayed. On the eve of his crucifixion, Jesus took his disciples to the upper room, where he proceeded to wash their feet in love and give them the bread and the wine of their first Communion. That night he gave his friends the remarkable promise that by faith in him, in answer to the prayer they offered to his Father in heaven, they would do even greater works than he had done. In saying this, Jesus put strong emphasis on obedience to God. "If you love me," he said, "you will keep my commandments" (John 14:15).

Back at Simon's house, in response to the woman who poured her perfume on his feet, Jesus had connected love to forgiveness. On that occasion he emphasized the *affective* (or emotional) dimension of love—the response of a forgiven heart. Here he connects love forward to obedience and emphasizes the *practical* dimension of love—the response of an obedient life.

The disciples could not keep God's commandments

in their own strength, of course, but only by the powerful presence of the Holy Spirit, who fills our lives with
God's love. So as soon as Jesus told his disciples that obedience would be the proof of their love, he proceeded to
give them this promise: "I will ask the Father, and he will
give you another Helper, to be with you forever, even the
Spirit of truth, whom the world cannot receive, because it
neither sees him nor knows him. You know him, for he
dwells with you and will be in you. I will not leave you as
orphans; I will come to you" (John 14:16–18). With these
words, Jesus promised that his Spirit would be the power
of obedience for a life of Christlike love. We learned this
back in chapter 1, when we looked at Romans 5: God pours
his love into our hearts through the Holy Spirit.

Before the Spirit could come, Jesus had to complete his
saving work. So even though the disciples hardly understood it, Jesus alluded to his impending death and resurrection and to the life that would always be theirs as a
result: "Yet a little while and the world will see me no
more, but you will see me. Because I live, you also will
live. In that day you will know that I am in my Father, and
you in me, and I in you" (vv. 19–20).

But soon Jesus returned to the theme of loving obedience: "Whoever has my commandments and keeps them,
he it is who loves me. And he who loves me will be loved
by my Father, and I will love him and manifest myself
to him" (v. 21). Then, in response to a question from one
of his disciples, Jesus repeated himself: "If anyone loves

me, he will keep my word, and my Father will love him, and we will come to him and make our home with him. Whoever does not love me does not keep my words. And the word that you hear is not mine but the Father's who sent me" (vv. 23–24).

Notice what gets reiterated all the way through this passage. Jesus began in verse 15 by saying that if we love him, we will keep his commandments. In verse 21 he flipped that around and said that keeping his commandments is a clear and obvious sign that we really do love him. Then in verse 23 he went back to what he said in verse 15, using slightly different words to say basically the same thing: "If anyone loves me, he will keep my word." Finally, in verse 24, he expressed the same principle in negative terms. The characteristic of people who do *not* love Jesus is that they refuse to do what he says.

In each case, there is a clear connection between keeping the commands of Christ and showing affection to Christ, between loving and obeying Jesus. By repeating himself so many times, Jesus added triple exclamation marks to this principle. This helps to ensure that we do not miss what he is saying: one of the best ways for us to show our love for Jesus is simply to do what he says.

Fathers and mothers understand this principle well. Joyful obedience is one of the fastest ways to a parent's heart. By contrast, failing to follow clear instructions is a sign of disaffection as well as disrespect—something I tried to explain to my daughter one time when we were discussing the difference between a clean bunny rabbit cage and a dirty bunny rabbit cage. Love is as love does.

The Law of Love

The connection Jesus makes between love and obedience gives us a true standard for love. It is strange to say, but people sometimes set love in opposition to the law of God. They say we should do the loving thing, which sounds good until it becomes apparent that some of the things they support in the name of love are unlawful to Jesus Christ. Then love itself becomes an excuse to endorse immoral behavior, for example, or to refuse to confront somebody's prejudice. Actually, the loving thing to do is to address sin, not ignore it, but sometimes people avoid an issue because confrontation doesn't seem like the loving thing to do.

Love never stands in opposition to the law of God, but always expresses its ultimate principles. Consider the two greatest commandments that Jesus ever gave. Both of them are based on love: love for God and love for neighbor.

Then take those two commandments and break them out into the Ten Commandments. The first four are all about love for God: love for his supremacy ("Don't have any other gods"), his worship ("Don't use idols"), his name ("Don't take it in vain"), and his day ("Remember the Sabbath"). The last six commandments are all about showing love to other people, starting with our parents. We are called to love people's life ("Don't murder"), purity ("Don't commit adultery"), property ("Don't steal"), reputation ("Don't bear false witness"), and prosperity ("Don't covet").

True love always stands in conformity to the commands of Christ. The loving thing is the lawful thing. So when people make an argument for affirming this practice or condoning that behavior on the basis of love, we have a clear standard for evaluating their argument: Is what they advocate in keeping with the commands of Christ? Because if we love him, we will keep his commandments.

How to Say "I Love You"

Here is how one commentator summarized what Jesus said about love in John 14: "Love is the foundation of obedience, and obedience is the sure outcome and result of love."[1] Another commentator put it this way: "Obedience is a certain inevitable consequence of affection for Christ."[2] Or we could simply say it like this: to love is to obey, and to obey is to love.

This principle is well illustrated in famous lines from *The Princess Bride*. In the film nothing gave the fair princess, Buttercup, more pleasure than giving orders to Westley, the farm boy. "Polish the saddle," she commanded. "Fill these with water." "Fetch me that pitcher." All Westley ever said in reply was, "As you wish," and then he did whatever his princess demanded. Then one day Buttercup realized that Westley's words were more than mere courtesy. She discovered, to her amazement, that when he said, "As you wish," what he really meant was, "I love you."

We say the same thing to Jesus whenever we do whatever he tells us to do out of sincere devotion to him. The "as you wish" of our obedience is the "I love you" of a life that is offered to Christ.

Our goal in this book is to grow in our affection for Jesus. There is an emotional dimension to love, of course, as we learned from the woman who anointed Jesus with her tears. But when Jesus told his disciples how to love him, the main thing he talked about was not a feeling in the heart, but the obedience of a life.

As we have seen in John, Jesus repeatedly demands obedience of his disciples. But the connection between love and obedience appears in other places as well. For example, in his discourse on the vine and the branches, Jesus said, "If you keep my commandments, you will abide in my love" (John 15:10). As a beloved disciple (e.g., John 20:2; 21:7), John learned this lesson well and repeated it in some of his other writings. Here is how "we know that we have come to know him," John said, "if we keep his commandments" (1 John 2:3); "whoever keeps his word, in him truly the love of God is perfected" (2:5). John wrote something similar near the end of the same epistle: "This is the love of God, that we keep his commandments" (5:3). He said it again in his second epistle: "This is love, that we walk according to his commandments" (2 John 1:6).

These passages are especially important to remember

when we do not feel especially loving toward Jesus, or when we are not sure what loving Jesus feels like at all. His main priority for our love is not a particular emotion (which may come and go), but practical obedience to his revealed will.

A Thousand Ways to Love

Knowing that love is as love does gives us a thousand down-to-earth ways to love Jesus more. One place to find a good list is in the Community Covenant of Wheaton College. This Covenant binds every student, professor, staff member, and trustee to a lifestyle of faithfulness to Jesus Christ. Like most of the covenants that people made in biblical times, at its heart the Community Covenant is a promise to love: "love for God, acted out in love for others, in obedience to God's Word." The commitments people on Wheaton's campus make to one another—and to God—are expressions of affection.

As a member of Wheaton College, the Community Covenant gives me many ways to love. I mention some of them here because they really apply to any Christian. For example, the Community Covenant calls me to exercise careful stewardship of my time, possessions, abilities, and opportunities. So whenever I adjust my agenda to serve someone else rather than myself, or give what I have to the poor, or use my mind to think wisely and carefully about a complex issue, I am saying "I love you" to Jesus.

The Community Covenant also calls me to participate in the life of the local church. So whenever I go to a worship service and sing God's praise, or listen to the preaching of God's Word, or teach a Sunday school class—as long as I am doing these things with a true heart for God—I am telling Jesus "I love you" all over again.

To give yet another example, Wheaton's Community Covenant calls me to be "a person of integrity whose word can be fully trusted." So whenever I follow through on a hard commitment rather than putting it off, and whenever I put myself in a true light rather than a better light, my integrity is a love message to my Savior.

I once received an encouraging letter from one of the college's neighbors. Apparently, one of our students lost control of his bike, crashed into a parked car, and left a big scratch across the back. What the neighbor wanted me to see was the note that the student left on his car, taking responsibility for the accident, giving contact information, and asking the neighbor please to call so that he could make things right. Hopefully, the student also recognized his need to work on his cycling skills, but at least his heart was in the right place: speaking the truth rather than keeping things secret is a demonstration of love for Christ.

There are thousands of ways to love Jesus more. As Wheaton's Community Covenant rightly says, "Christ-like love should be the motive in all decisions, actions, and relationships." Exercising responsible Christian freedom, doing honest work, treating people's bodies with honor, seeking mercy and justice for the oppressed, upholding the sanctity of life, promoting biblical principles for marriage, sharing the gospel—this is what love does. These are all ways of loving Jesus more, not just at Wheaton College, but anywhere.

The Jesus Way to Love

Too often we think of obedience as a joyless duty or a legalistic demand. Jesus liberates us by teaching us to think of obedience as our loving response to his loving grace. Our Father in heaven does not go around saying, "Just do as I say" all the time. Instead, he invites us to offer obedience from the heart as a gift of our love. David Watson says it like this: "God's love language to us is mercy and grace. Our love language to God is loving obedience."[3]

One college student who wanted to encourage his classmates in the grace of God wrote to me about his struggle with perfectionism. Maybe you can relate to what he said:

When we focus all our attention on looking good on the outside we miss the way God intended our relationship with him and each other to be. . . . Yes, I struggle, I sin. I have evil thoughts, I judge people, I am extremely selfish, and I am tempted. When we can resist these things because we so understand God's love for us and know that He wants the best for us—this is the reason we shouldn't be sinning, not to have a checklist of things not to do.

Obedience to God is not a checklist of things not to do (or even a checklist of things *to* do), but a loving response to a loving Savior. Cyril of Alexandria, who was among the wisest fathers of the early Christian church, said it like this: "Keeping the divine commandments is the best way to give living expression to our love toward God."[4]

The person who knows this best is Jesus himself. Everything he ever did when he lived on this earth was a demonstration of love—love for his Father and love for us. In love Jesus came down from heaven. In love he was born in poverty and obscurity. In love he served his parents, honoring his father and mother. In love he always did what his heavenly Father wanted him to do. "I have kept my Father's commandments," Jesus said, "and abide in his love" (John 15:10; cf. Heb. 10:7).

In love Jesus went to Gethsemane and then on to Calvary. The way he prayed to his Father in that dreary garden proves that his crucifixion was an act of obedience. After wrestling with the possibility of a wrath-free atonement, he said, "Your will be done" (Matt. 26:42). In going to the cross Jesus was keeping covenant with his ancient promise to do everything that needed to be done for our salvation. The sufferings of the cross were the supreme statement of the Son's love for the Father, and for us.

The crucifixion secures our salvation. It also means that Jesus has firsthand knowledge of the vital connection between obedience and love. So when he tells us that to love is to obey—when he says that love is as love does—he is inviting us to follow him in a life of loving obedience to the Father.

When she was eight years old, my daughter Karoline surprised me one day by saying, "Dad, do you remember that day when you were just like Jesus?"

Actually, I couldn't remember a day like that. To tell the truth, a wave of something like grief washed over me as I realized that there had never been a day like that in my entire life—a day when I was just like Jesus. Still, I was curious to find out what day she had in mind, in case there might have been a day when I was at least a little bit like Jesus.

"*You* know," she said, with amused exasperation, "on your birthday, when you told us that the only thing you wanted was to get us our bunnies. That was just like Jesus—sacrificing yourself for us."

Honestly, that is basically what birthdays are like when a father of five turns forty-six years old. You do not get to do what you want to do; you do what needs to be done for everybody else (in this case, delivering on a promise that was almost two months late). But maybe Karoline was right: what I did for her was a little bit like Jesus. And I realized that when I followed his example of obedient love, I wasn't just saying "I love you" to my daughters. I had found another way to say "I love you" to Jesus, which is easy to do, because there are so many ways to do it.

6

Love's Greatest Test

I well remember the sense of euphoria I felt when my doctoral dissertation was approved and I knew that I would never have to take another academic examination ever again. Of course, three months later I was up for ordination and I had to pass exams in Greek, Hebrew, English Bible, church history, systematic theology, sacraments, and church government. When it comes to examining candidates for pastoral ministry, Presbyterians are nothing if not thorough!

The reality is that whether or not we happen to be in school, life is full of tests, both large and small. The most important examinations are spiritual, like the one we will consider in this chapter. What do you suppose is the greatest test of your love for Jesus Christ? The answer might surprise you.

Where Jesus Was Tested

We begin in a dark place—a place of severe temptation, heart-breaking pain, and the deepest agony of an innocent soul. We begin in Gethsemane.

It was the night before Christ was crucified, and he had gone with some of his best friends to one of his favorite places—a little grove on the Mount of Olives. It was the dark night of our Savior's soul, when he was "sorrowful, even to death" (Matt. 26:38). In such extreme anguish that he was sweating blood (Luke 22:44), Jesus asked his Father if there was any alternative to the cross.

The answer was no. Jesus could only save us by offering a blood sacrifice for our sins. So he went from Gethsemane to Calvary, where he poured out the last full measure of his blood for sinners.

If we ask why Jesus did this, the answer is that he did it for love. "God shows his love for us," the Bible says, "in that while we were still sinners, Christ died for us" (Rom. 5:8). "By this we know love, that he laid down his life for us" (1 John 3:16). "Christ loved the church, and gave himself up for her" (Eph. 5:25). At the hour of his greatest testing, Jesus chose to love his people to the death of his body and the sacrifice of his soul.

Each of us faces a lesser test in which God calls us to make a similar choice and to love the church that Jesus loves. This may be the truest test of our love for our Lord: will we go out and love the church that he died to save?

People Who Are Hard to Love

We need to be honest about how hard it is to love the church. To begin with, the church has people in it, and people are hard to love. Honestly, I find it hard enough to love anyone. But some people are harder to love than others, and some of the people who are the hardest to love call themselves Christians.

We tend to have high expectations for other believers—higher than we have for people who do not know Christ—so when they fail to live up to our standards, it is tempting to get angry or cynical. Perhaps we thought that in joining the church or connecting in some other way to the body of Christ we were entering a healthy community. Yet sometimes we are surprised by sin. We see the reality gap between what people say they believe and how they actually live, and this disconnect makes some people very hard for us to love. We will have the same experience in any church we attend or Christian community we ever visit: disciples of Christ who disappoint us. This is disillusioning, disheartening, and makes it downright difficult to love the church.

Then there are all the disagreements we have in theology. Some Christians interpret the Bible differently than we do. Even when we more or less agree with their doctrine, we do not always appreciate their attitude. Political disagreements can be even worse. Sometimes we get embarrassed by the way other Christians connect their faith to public life.

Other times it is mainly a matter of style. We do not particularly care for the way that some Christians do church, or share the gospel, or worship God, or understand the relationship between Christianity and culture. To tell the truth, some Christians are harder for us to love than people who are totally outside the church.

It is sometimes said that Jesus has endured three humiliations. The first was the humiliation of the incarnation, when God the Son was born in a stable, becoming a human being. The second was when he died on the cross, with all its curse and shame. But his third humiliation is sometimes overlooked: the community we call the body of Christ, which he left behind to do his work in the world.

It is doubtful whether most of us would want to have our name permanently connected to something as deeply flawed as the church, or that we would leave something as important as world evangelization in the hands of fallen sinners, but this is precisely what Jesus has done.

Our Savior calls us to have the same love for the church that he has, which is a real test for us. In fact, this is one of the main ways we love Jesus more: by loving his people, the church.

Do You Love Me?

To see what it means to love Jesus by loving the church, we go to a happier place—not to the garden of Gethsemane, but to the shores of Galilee. John 21 tells the story of a fishing expedition that took place sometime after the resurrection of Jesus Christ. Peter, who was always the ringleader, announced that he was going fishing, and some of the other disciples decided to go with him. They fished all night, but caught nothing—something that happens so often in the Gospels that one wonders how the disciples ever made a living as fishermen!

At the first light of day a stranger on the shore told them to cast their nets on the other side. They caught such a huge draft of fish that they couldn't even haul them into the boat. Peter immediately recognized that the stranger had to be Jesus. He leaped from the boat and swam to shore. The other disciples dragged in their nets, and they all enjoyed the best fish fry ever: 153 fish over an open fire with the Savior of the world.

After breakfast a remarkable conversation took place, in which Jesus tenderly performed open heart surgery on one of his closest disciples. He began by questioning Peter's affections: "Simon, son of John, do you love me more than these?"

Jesus was asking a question in the form of a comparison. It is not entirely clear what he meant by "more than these." Maybe he was referring to the other disciples. Peter had claimed that even if all the other disciples fell away, he would never leave Jesus. Or maybe Jesus was referring to the tools of the fishing trade, the nets and the boats which Peter seemed to have picked up again. Did this disciple love Jesus more than his former calling as a fisherman? Or perhaps

Jesus was making a more global comparison. Whatever else he may have loved, did Peter love Jesus more than anything?

In any case, Peter was being asked if he loved Jesus more. The fisherman answered with a strong affirmation of his affection: "Yes, Lord; you know that I love you" (John 21:15, 16). Peter was so certain of his love for Jesus that he appealed to our Lord's own conscience. Peter knew that he was in love with Jesus, and he knew that Jesus knew it too.

Once Peter had pledged his love, Jesus gave him a clear and simple command: "Feed my lambs" (John 21:15). As the conversation continued, he reiterated these instructions, with slightly different phrasing: "Tend my sheep" (v. 16); "Feed my sheep" (v. 17). If it was true that Peter loved Jesus, he would live out that love in the church by serving the people of God.

This conversation was part of Peter's unique calling as an apostle. But it is recorded in John's Gospel so that we can listen in and learn what applies to us. Jesus asks each of us the same question that he asked Peter, and gives each of us a similar calling: "Do you love me? Do you love me *more*: more than your friends, more than your work, more than your old way of life? If you do, then you will love my people so much that you will go out and use your gifts to serve them."

Who Is Called to Love the Church?

Notice who is called to love Jesus by loving his sheep: someone who failed Jesus by denying him. In talking to Peter, Jesus was questioning the affection and demanding the service of a man who totally rejected him the night before his crucifixion.

Remember the backstory to this breakfast. Only a short time before, Peter had been warming himself at another fire, in the courtyard of the high priest. On that sad night, as the Son of Man went through the show trial that led to his execution, Peter publicly denied that he had any connection to Jesus—not once, but three times.

This triple denial fulfilled the famous prophecy that Jesus made about Peter and the rooster (see Matt. 26:34). It also explains Peter's intense emotional reaction when Jesus asked him for the third time, "Simon, son of John, do you love me?" (John 21:17). This was a moment of high drama. By repeating his question, and then repeating it again, Jesus was calling to mind Peter's three denials.

As soon as he heard the same question for the third time, Peter knew what Jesus meant. The Bible indicates that he "was grieved because he said to him the third time, 'Do you love me?'" Peter knew that Jesus had every right to question his affection. How could someone who had failed to live for Jesus honestly claim to love him? Yet Peter had to be true to his own heart. So he said, "Lord, you know everything; you know that I love you" (John 21:17).

This exchange shows that even if we have failed Jesus in all kinds of ways, he still desires our affection and wants to have a relationship with us. The call to love Jesus by loving the church is not for people who love Jesus perfectly and never struggle to love other Christians. It is for fickle people who have failed rather badly, even to the point of denying the Son of God.

There is more than a little Peter in most of us. All of us are failed disciples. We get opportunities to give a strong witness to the gospel, but lack the courage to speak up, and the moment quickly passes us by. We sin against God, sometimes against our better judgment. We confess our sins and receive forgiveness, but the fact remains that we have denied our Savior.

Some of us deny Jesus by failing to live up to the shared commitments of his church. We neglect the Word and the worship of God. We give in to pride, or indulge in gossip, or are guilty of hypocrisy. We keep a place in our lives for racial prejudice or sexual sin, or we abuse the good things of life in ways that are dishonoring to God.

If any of this is true of us—if we have denied Jesus, and may deny him again—we should know that Jesus loves us. He desires our love in return, and will always be ready to receive us with open arms.

So we should consider what answer we would give to the question that Jesus asked Peter. He wants to know: "Do you love me?" If we are able to give the answer that Peter gave—"Yes, Lord; you know that I love you"—then we will prove it by loving the church that Jesus loves.

Why We Should Love the Church

In fulfilling the call of Christ to love the church, it helps to have a compelling motivation for treating our relationship with his people as a lifelong romance. Our motivation is simply this: we love the church because Jesus loved it enough to die for it.

A college student once wrote to me about his struggle with God's standards for human sexuality. He knew there were things the Bible said are wrong, but some people think are right, and part of him wished he could just ignore what the Bible said. Furthermore, he found other Christians to be so judgmental that it was turning him off to Christianity. But he also found the love of God drawing him back. Here is what he wrote:

> I need to truly find love in my heart for God's people again. Loving [non-Christians] is of no merit; it takes nothing. Coexisting with other Christians is an enormous challenge. Loving the church is impossible. But God did it. The language to describe God's love for the church is deeply passionate—almost erotic. The only way for me to have that love is to receive it directly from someone else. Otherwise, it is truly impossible.

When people are hard for us to love, we tend to think that they are to blame, but really the problem is us. It's not just that they are hard to love; it's also that we are not very loving, which is why we need more of God's love in our lives.

The metaphor that Jesus used to describe how he wanted Peter to love the church reminds us of the extent of his saving love. His imagery in these instructions is all about tending flocks and feeding sheep. The Savior who spoke these words frequently styled himself as a shepherd. Jesus is the shepherd who came to seek and to save the lost. He will go out into the mountains to find and rescue even one lost sheep. Then he leads his sheep beside quiet waters and comforts them in the valley of the shadow of death. He speaks to them so they know his voice. Most of all, Jesus is the shepherd who gives his life for the sheep.

We may not always be very impressed with the church. All too often, we get frustrated with other Christians. We are embarrassed by what they do, or fail to do. In fact, sometimes they are the hardest people in the world to love. But we should never forget that Jesus loves these people so much that he gave up his life for them.

How to Love the Church

Now Jesus calls us to love his people with a shepherd's love, and to love them as much as he does: "By this we know love, that he laid down his life for us, and we ought to lay down our lives for the brothers" (1 John 3:16; cf. John 13:34). There are all kinds of ways to do this. If we love Jesus more, then active involvement in a local congregation will be one of our main commitments in life. One of our first priorities when we move to a new place to start a new job, take up a new station, or attend a new school is to find the God-worshiping, Bible-teaching, gospel-sharing, world-serving church where God wants us to belong.

If we love Jesus, we will not think exclusively or even primarily about what that church can do for us, but about what God is calling us to do in that church—how he wants us to use our gifts and get involved in its ministry. Once I visited a recent alumnus of Wheaton College who was working at a Christian school in Chicago. He told me that he was moving into an apartment only a few blocks from his church. He wanted to live close enough so that he wouldn't have any excuse not getting involved in the worship, ministry, and fellowship of his local congregation. I told him that he was making the wisest decision a young single man in the city could make. He was putting Jesus first in his heart by putting the church first in his life. In doing so, he was setting out on a trajectory of lifelong service to God.

Loving the church that Jesus loves means being faithful in worship. Here Jesus is the perfect example. If anyone could have said that he had such a close relationship with God that he didn't need the church, it was God the Son. Yet again and again we see him going to the synagogue or the temple for worship. He said to his Father, "I will tell of your name to my brothers; in the midst of the congregation I will sing your praise" (Heb. 2:12; cf. Ps. 22:22). If it was important for Jesus to worship with the people of God, it is certainly important for us.

Loving the church that Jesus loves means going deeper in friendships with brothers and sisters in Christ. This requires a high degree of intentionality. Christ-centered community does not come to us; we have to go out and find it, and then become part of growing it. We should not neglect meeting with other Christians, which is a bad habit that some people get into, but encourage our brothers and sisters every chance we get (see Heb. 10:25).

Loving the church also means this: offering our lives in service to others. Peter did this by feeding God's flock. He was called to be a shepherd, which is really another word for pastor. Our calling may be different. We may work in the nursery, teach a Bible study, lead music in worship, direct a youth ministry, feed the homeless, or care for the disabled.

When I was in pastoral ministry at a local church, the people I counted on the most served God faithfully week after week, never complaining about how difficult it was or envying the gifts of others, but cheerfully doing whatever God called them to do. I think of Roy Oliver, who had an encouraging word for me after every one of my first sermons (some of which were pretty bad). I think of Sheryl Woods Olsen, the world-class opera singer who faithfully brought a severely disabled friend to church whenever she was in town. I think of Arlita Winston, who led our pastors' wives through a full day of sharing, prayer, and Bible study every month. I think of Howard Blair, who in his 70s and 80s kept traveling overseas to teach the Bible to other pastors. Reverend Blair told me that the older he got, the more he enjoyed his life with Jesus. "It gets better and better!" he said.

Each of us has our own gifts to share, and we will find God's pleasure as we put them to use in the ministry of the church. Of course, God is also calling us to use our gifts in the wider world. But he is not calling us to do this all by ourselves. He is calling us to serve Christ and his kingdom through the hard-to-love community that the Bible calls the church.

Final Examination

So this is our test: loving Jesus by loving his people. Peter passed this test. At the end of their conversation by the Sea of Galilee, Jesus said, "Follow me" (John 21:19). Peter then followed him all the way to the end of his life, when he fulfilled the prophecy of Jesus (v. 18) and died to the glory of God. Will we join Peter in doing the difficult, costly thing that God is calling us to do and give our lives to the church that Jesus loves?

Earlier in this chapter I quoted a student who found it almost impossible to love other Christians. But then he remembered the love of Jesus, which actually makes it possible for us to love. Here is what the student went on to say:

God's love is impossible, without God. Love is an impossible thing to be given and received by us. But through God's love, he made his love within the realm of possibility once more. His impossible love is not a standard. It is an ocean. We cannot explore it, question its power, dam up its might, or explore its deep. We can only be washed over by it.

When God's love washes over us, it becomes possible for us to pass the greatest test of our affections and grow in our "love toward the Lord Jesus and for all the saints" (Philem. 1:5).

7

When I Don't
Love Jesus

Mark Guy Pearse was a Methodist minister from Cornwall, on the southwest coast of England. This was back in the nineteenth century, and by all accounts Pearse was an exceptional preacher with a warm affection for his church members, including children. After one worship service a little girl came to him, looked up into his face quite wistfully, and said, "Mr. Pearse, I don't love Jesus. I wish I did love Jesus, but I don't love Jesus. Won't you please tell me how to love Jesus."[1]

We have been working on the same question in this book, trying to learn how to love Jesus more. So far we have learned that the source of our love for Jesus is not in us; love is a gift of the Holy Spirit, whom God pours into our hearts. We have seen that our strongest motivation for loving Jesus with everything we have is that he loves us with everything *he* has. We have seen how important it is for us to fight for the assurance of our faith. Whenever we have our doubts, we need to go back to the gospel, where Jesus tells us the love story of our salvation.

We have also considered the connection between love and forgiveness: the people who love Jesus most extravagantly are like the woman who anointed the feet of Jesus with sorry tears and sweet perfume: they know how many of their sins have been forgiven. And we have seen that love is as love does; the best test of our affection for Jesus is obedience to his instruction, including his command to love the church for which he died.

Yet even after everything we have learned, many of us can still relate to the little girl who said, "Please tell me how to love Jesus." Maybe we *wish* that we loved Jesus, but we do not love him as much as we should. This is a serious problem. Thomas Vincent began his exceptional book about loving the "unseen Christ" by describing the tragic implications of living without love. "The life of Christianity," he claimed, "consists very much in our love to Christ. Without love to Christ, we are as much without spiritual life as a carcass when the soul is fled from it is without natural life. Faith without love to Christ is a dead faith, and a Christian without love to Christ is a dead Christian, dead in sins and trespasses."[2] Jesus gave sober warnings about people who abandoned their first love (Rev. 2:4–5; cf. 1 Cor. 16:22). Surely something needs to be done about our loveless hearts! What then should we do when we don't love Jesus?

A Question of Salvation

We can understand the problem of a loveless heart better by looking at a famous conversation that is recounted in three of the four Gospels—the conversation Jesus had with the man commonly known as "the rich young ruler."

The term *ruler* (Gk. *archon*) comes from Luke's account of this incident. It does not necessarily mean that the man had a formal position in government, but at the very least he was a leader in his local community—a person of privilege. Later we learn that he was "extremely rich" (Luke 18:23). What this wealthy man wanted to do was admirable: he wanted to enter the kingdom of God. So he asked Jesus, "Good Teacher, what must I do to inherit eternal life?" (v. 18).

Unfortunately, the man was off on the wrong track already, because he was thinking of salvation as something he could get by something he did. Notice his question: "What must I *do* to inherit eternal life?" Here was a man who had worked hard for everything he had, and who expected therefore to pay full price for eternal life. To quote what he said more literally, "Having done what, will I inherit eternal life?" The implication was that he could merit salvation by something he did.

So how did Jesus answer? The truth is that anyone who wants to be saved by doing must keep every last one of God's laws (see Gal. 3:12). So Jesus said, "You know the commandments: 'Do not commit adultery, Do not murder, Do not steal, Do not bear false witness, Honor your father and mother'" (Luke 18:20). In other words, if you want to be saved by what you do, then keep the Ten Commandments! Jesus mentioned only five of them here, but in effect he was saying that they all have to be kept. God's perfect law demands our perfect obedience.

In his own humble opinion, the ruler had met this standard. So he claimed, "All these I have kept from my youth" (Luke 18:21). Really, the man was saying something like this: "The Ten Commandments? Is that all there is to it? Everyone knows that you have to keep *those*. In fact, I've been keeping them all my life!"

The man's response was as common then as it is today, when many people think of the Ten Commandments as a short list of bad sins they almost never commit. As a result, they think they can keep God's law well enough to satisfy God enough to get into heaven.

The problem with this way of thinking, of course, is that what God's law truly requires is not so simple. According to Jesus, each commandment rules our hearts as well as our actions. The command not to kill is about hatred, not just about murder. The command not to commit adultery isn't just about whom we touch, and where; it's also about the way we look at someone. And so on (see Matt. 5:21–28).

But if God's standard is inward as well as outward perfection, then how could the rich young ruler claim a lifetime of law-keeping? Had he never said anything that wasn't completely true, or cherished an idol in his heart, or uttered a single profanity (even if no one else heard it)?

And what about us? We like people to admire us, but if they could read our true thoughts—if our inner dialogue got posted on Facebook, for example, with all our unkind thoughts and unholy desires—we would be ruined. We are not the good, true hobbits that we want people to think we are. There is an inner Gollum inside every one of us: a specter of grasping depravity, who lives only for our precious selves.

The Test of Love

Jesus did not expose the rich young ruler's pretensions to holiness by disputing his claim to sinless perfection, but instead by giving him one simple test. If the man really was keeping the commandments, then obviously he was keeping the law that demanded his primary affection: "You shall have no other gods before me" (Ex. 20:3). So, was God first in the man's life, or not? Was he giving all his love to God, or was something else getting in the way? Jesus tested him by saying, "One thing you still lack. Sell all that you have and distribute to the poor, and you will have treasure in heaven; and come, follow me" (Luke 18:22).

Whereas some rabbis of the day set a limit on giving to the poor, Jesus told the rich young ruler to sell everything and give away all the proceeds. In making this demand, he was not saying that we can win our way to heaven simply by giving away all our wealth. No, the requirement for salvation is faith in Jesus Christ. But in this particular case, Jesus identified the one area of the ruler's life where he refused to love God. The man was willing to keep some of the commandments, but not to give up his standard of living for the glory of God, or to give up the social position that came with his wealth. Nick Perrin comments that for this man "to choose insolvency for the sake of joining Jesus' movement was to choose a kind of social death."[3] But the rich young ruler wasn't ready to make such a sacrifice. He loved the good life more than eternal life, and this was keeping him from loving Jesus.

In his early travels to America, the evangelist John Wesley stayed with a wealthy plantation owner. It took hours for him to tour the man's vast estate on horseback, yet even then he saw only a fraction of the man's property. At the end of the day the two men sat down to dinner. The plantation owner asked, "Well, Mr. Wesley, what do you think?" Wesley replied, "I think you're going to have a hard time leaving all this."[4]

The rich young ruler had the same difficulty, so Jesus told the man to give it all away. By selling his possessions, he would not be adding one more act of religious piety to his list of good deeds, but subtracting everything that was standing in the way of loving Jesus. It was not simply this asset or that asset that demanded divestiture. The man needed to eliminate everything in his life that was keeping him from Jesus. And in his particular case, this meant giving away everything he had.

What do you suppose that Jesus would tell *you* to give up for the kingdom of God? The answer is very simple. Would you like to know what it is? Maybe not! Honestly, most of us would rather make our own decisions about what to keep and what to give away. But Jesus would tell us to give up anything that we love more than we love him.

Sadly, the rich young ruler failed this test. Luke tells us that "when he heard these things, he became very sad, for he was extremely rich" (Luke 18:23). It wasn't just how much stuff he had that was the problem, however; it was the tightness of his grip. We know this because of his emotional reaction to the command of Christ. If Jesus was his first and highest love, then he would have been happy to pay any price to follow him. But he wasn't happy about it at all. According to Mark, the man was so sad that he left Jesus instead of following him (Mark 10:22).

Alternative Affections

Understand that there is only room in anyone's heart for one, single, overarching affection. What is your true love? We were born to love, and if we do not love Jesus the most, then there must be something or someone else that we love more than him.

If we started to write down all of the things that people love more than Jesus, it would be easy to generate a very long list. But maybe the best summary appears in Paul's second letter to Timothy, where the apostle mentions three unholy affections that will be common in the last days before the second coming of Jesus Christ. What will people love in the end times? According to Paul, they will love pleasure, money, and themselves (2 Tim. 3:2, 4). All three of these affections are easily recognized as dominating the human heart in the twenty-first century: hedonism, materialism, and narcissism.

Is it possible that one of these life-dominating affections explains why we do not love Jesus more? Maybe it's *hedonism*—the love of pleasure. We are immersed in a culture which insists that every fleshly desire should be gratified, and no physical enjoyment denied. To give just one example, Taco Bell ran a commercial during the 2013 Super Bowl in which a posse of senior citizens partied until dawn. It was meant to be a parody, of course, but the parody only works in a culture that lives for pleasure.

If our own lives are oriented toward the next sexual release, or the buzz that comes from drinking alcohol, or from gratifying some more sophisticated desire, then our love for pleasure is getting in the way of our love for Jesus. These are all ways of "making provision for the flesh," as Paul called it (Rom. 13:14).

Then again, maybe we love the same thing that the rich young ruler loved: money, and all the things it can buy. We have been seduced by *materialism*. So when we read what Jesus said to this young man—that he needed to give away everything he had—we are quick to point out that Jesus was speaking specifically to him and not necessarily to us.

That is true, of course, but why do we secretly hope that Jesus will never tell us to sell all *our* possessions and give to the poor? It must be because we are mastered by money.

Or maybe we love ourselves—the sin of *narcissism*. In Greek mythology, Narcissus was the beautiful youth who fell in love with his own reflection. As he sat beside a pool and gazed longingly at his image, he was transformed into a flower. That ancient myth is a story for our times, when being self-centered is considered practically a virtue. In his landmark study *The Culture of Narcissism*, sociologist Christopher Lasch discovered that ordinary Americans now display many of the character traits traditionally associated with pathological personality disorders. Narcissism has become normal.[5]

We live in a culture of takers, not givers. We want to live for ourselves, not for God. For a long time, this is what kept C. S. Lewis from coming to Christ. He wanted to be his own Ultimate Authority, but Christianity would not allow this. "There was," he wrote, "no region even in the innermost depth of one's soul . . . which one could surround with a barbed wire fence and guard with a notice 'No Admittance.' And that was what I wanted; some area, however small, of which I could say to all other beings, 'This is my business and mine only.'"[6]

Hedonism, materialism, narcissism: these are some of the many loves that keep us from loving Jesus. Loving him more always requires us to love other things less. Yet sometimes this is the very last thing that we want to do. Consider these haunting words from the Anglican bishop J. C. Ryle: "Many are ready to give up everything for Christ's sake, excepting one darling sin, and for the sake of that sin are lost."[7] What is your darling sin—the one thing you will not give up for Jesus? Is there any sin you will not renounce, any relationship you will not release, any treasure you will not relinquish to follow Jesus? Whatever that one thing is, it explains why you don't love Jesus more.

Hope for the Loveless

There is still hope for us, however, and we find that hope at the end of the story. Although for the rich young ruler it turned out to be a tragedy (as far as we know), for us it can still have a happy ending.

The story is tragic because the man's love of money prevented him from following Jesus. When Jesus told him to sell all his possessions and give everything to the poor, he sadly walked away from the Savior of the world. Yet the things that Jesus said and felt at the end of this story open up the hope of salvation—even for people like us, who are tempted to live for an alternative affection.

Mark tells us that when the young man first announced that he had kept all of God's commandments, "Jesus, looking at him, loved him" (Mark 10:21). Undoubtedly, this is the *last* thing most of us would have done. If there is one kind of person we find it hard to love, it is someone who is so self-righteous that he thinks he never sins! But (thank

God) Jesus has as much compassion for the proud legalist as he does for any poor sinner.

Luke confirms this by showing us more of the loving heart of Jesus. He tells us that when the rich young ruler turned his back and walked away, Jesus looked at him again, not in anger, but with compassion. This gives amazing hope to anyone who has ever rejected Jesus for some other love. He does not respond by hating us, but by loving us.

Even better, Jesus continues to offer us eternal life. This is the direction he points in the comment he made while the rich young ruler was walking away. Turning to his disciples, he said, "How difficult it is for those who have wealth to enter the kingdom of God! For it is easier for a camel to go through the eye of a needle than for a rich person to enter the kingdom of God" (Luke 18:24–25).

Some preachers have tried to diminish the force of this statement by saying that when Jesus said "camel" he did not really mean "camel." They have said, for example, that there was a gate in Jerusalem—called the Needle Gate—that was too small for camels, so traders had to unload their animals before entering. This is an interesting suggestion, but there is no evidence to support it. Besides, it is really missing the point. Jesus wanted to show that humanly speaking, it is *impossible* for rich people to get saved. So he took the biggest animal that most people had ever seen and imagined trying to stuff it through the eye of a needle.

The disciples understood what Jesus meant right away, and they could hardly believe it. "Then who can be saved?" they asked (Luke 18:26). I mean, if rich people can't get into the kingdom, then how can anyone be saved? The assumption in those days was that wealthy people had God's blessing. But if Jesus was right, and it was impossible for them to get in, then what hope could there be for anyone?

Rather than denying the difficulty, Jesus agreed that it was impossible. But then he went on to make the promise of his grace: "What is impossible with man is possible with God" (v. 27).

It is practically a miracle when rich people come to Christ because it requires us to divest ourselves of our dependence on our wealth and to start trusting in God alone for our salvation.[8] But if we want the proof that God ever performs this miracle of grace, all we need to do is look at all the wealthy people in the Bible who believed in the Savior—people like Abraham and David, Boaz and Job, Esther and Lydia, Barnabas and Joseph of Arimathea. Jesus was right: "What is impossible with man *is* possible with God." On the basis of his death on the cross, his triumph over the tomb, and the powerful inward work of his Spirit, Jesus Christ is able to save the richest sinners.

Because He First Loved Me

The possibility of grace gives hope to all of us. Most of us have times when we doubt rather seriously that God would ever save someone like us. And maybe the reason we have our doubts is because some unholy affection is keeping us away from the love of Jesus. If so, then we need to know that Jesus still has a heart for us. He looks at us in love the way he looked at the rich young ruler. This is the amazing thing about his divine affection. Even when we don't love Jesus, he still loves us.

At the beginning of this chapter I introduced the little girl who went up to Mark Guy Pearse and said, "I don't love Jesus." Needless to say, the minister wanted to help her. So he looked down into her eager eyes and said, "Little girl, as you go home today keep saying to yourself, 'Jesus loves me. Jesus loves me. Jesus loves me.' And when you come back next Sunday I think you will be able to say, 'I love Jesus.'"

This is exactly what the little girl did; she kept telling herself, "Jesus loves me." When the minister saw her the next Sunday, her face was radiant and her eyes were dancing with joy. She ran up to him and said, "Oh, Mr. Pearse, I do love Jesus, I do love Jesus. Last Sunday as I went home I kept saying to myself, 'Jesus loves me. Jesus loves me. Jesus loves me.' And I began to think about his love and I began to think how he died on the cross in my place, and I found my cold heart growing warm, and the first I knew it was full of love to Jesus."[9]

When you don't love Jesus, remember that he still loves you, and that he is able to put his love into your loveless heart.

8

Sight Unseen

I wish I could see what Peter saw. As one of the original disciples, Peter was a daily eyewitness to Jesus Christ. He was a guest at the wedding in Cana when Jesus turned water into wine—his first miracle. He saw Jesus heal the sick, including Peter's own mother-in-law. He watched a group of friends break through the roof and drop a lame man into a crowded house where Jesus was teaching. Then he watched in amazement as the man stood up and walked.

These were not the only things that Peter saw. Peter witnessed almost everything we read about in the Gospels: the all-day sermons and late-night chat sessions, the crowds by the seashore and conflicts in Jerusalem, the mealtimes and the miracles. Oh, the stories that old fisherman could tell!

One dark night on the Sea of Galilee, when he was out fishing with his buddies, Peter saw Jesus walking toward him on the water—the Wave Master. Then there was the time he went up the mountain to pray and saw Jesus transfigured in radiant splendor—the Son of God in the white heat of divine glory. When the apostle later described this experience to others, he said, "We were eyewitnesses of his majesty" (2 Pet. 1:16).

At the end of it all, Peter saw Jesus go to the cross. In a matter of hours, he watched Jesus betrayed, arrested, beaten, tried, condemned, and crucified. Then, before he knew what had happened, Peter was running back to the grave, where the only thing he saw was a burial shroud, because Jesus was already gone. But Peter saw him again before the day was over: the risen Lord, Jesus Christ. Then a month and a half later he saw him for the last time on earth, as Jesus ascended to heaven and returned to his Father's glory.

These are all things that Peter saw with his own two eyes, as an eyewitness apostle. Don't you wish that you could see what Peter saw?

(Not) Seeing Is (Not) Believing

But we can't see what Peter saw. This is the challenge we face as people who live somewhere between the first advent and the second coming of Jesus Christ: we worship our Savior sight unseen.

Sometimes this causes us to have our doubts. Just ask Nathanael. His friend Philip had decided to follow Jesus (this was right at the beginning of our Lord's public ministry). When Philip claimed that he had found the Christ, Nathanael couldn't believe it. "Come and see," Philip said, but Nathanael didn't believe in Jesus until he met him in person and heard what he had to say. For Nathanael, seeing was believing.

The same thing was true for Thomas, of course—the most famous skeptic in the early church. Thomas was one of the original twelve disciples, but for some reason he was not with the others when Jesus appeared to them on the first Easter Sunday. For more than a week he insisted that he would not believe in the resurrection unless and until he could see Jesus for himself. Bible readers tend to be hard on Thomas, but I sympathize with the man. Like a disciplined scientist, or maybe a tough-minded philosopher, he demanded more evidence to warrant his belief. The more people pushed him to believe, the more he insisted on having better proof.

All it took for Thomas was one look at Jesus, standing there in his resurrection body, to answer every lingering question and silence every cynical doubt. "My Lord and my God!" the skeptic said. Jesus responded by pronouncing a blessing—not on Thomas, but for us: "Have you believed because you have seen me? Blessed are those who have not seen and yet have believed" (John 20:29). Believing without seeing has God's blessing.

The trouble is that many of us find it easier to believe what we can actually see. Like Thomas and Nathanael, we don't want to get fooled, so we insist on having more evidence before we are willing to put our total trust in Jesus—not only for salvation, but also in all our plans for the future.

We can't always see what God is doing, and this makes it hard for us to have faith. We are in the longest of all long-distance relationships, separated from God by time and eternity. No Skype. No Facebook. No text messages. We have the Bible, of course, but it doesn't always answer our questions very directly or give us the specific guidance we are looking for. We also have prayer, but some of our prayers go unanswered (at least it seems that way to us). In our suffering, we wonder if God really cares. We see dark places in the world—including our own hearts—where the gospel doesn't seem to make much difference. And when we can't really see how God is at work, we doubt he is really there.

As a result, many Christians worry about having a "Manti Te'o" moment in their spiritual lives. Football fans admired the Hawaiian-born Manti Te'o as an All-American linebacker at Notre Dame. Near the beginning of the 2012 college football season they were moved by stories of his tender devotion to his girlfriend back home, struggling with leukemia, and then shocked to learn of her sudden death in a fatal car accident. Yet the whole thing turned out to be an elaborate hoax. The young woman Te'o met online—supposedly named Lennay Kekua—never actually existed. So the All-American was humiliated publicly for believing in someone he had never seen and having a relationship with a person he had never met.

Sometimes we worry that the same thing could happen to us in our relationship with Jesus. We have been counting on him for eternal life, but what if the whole thing is a hoax? Maybe Jesus Christ is like Lennay Kekua, and like Manti Te'o we are caught in a bad romance. How can we be secure in the love of a Savior we have never seen? What if he never existed? What will we do then?

Worshiping an invisible Christ often seems like a problem for Christianity. It certainly seems that way to non-Christians. When the anthropologist Tanya Luhrmann wrote a book about evangelicals and their personal experience with God, she commented that outsiders think born-again believers are "out of touch with reality."[1] Skeptics wonder, "How can sensible, educated people believe in an invisible being who has a real effect on their lives?"[2]

This question is a test of our faith and a challenge for our evangelism. When the evangelical statesman Charles Colson addressed the Harvard Divinity School on the subject of Christian apologetics, he spent half his lecture giving evidence for the existence of God. Afterward, Professor Henri Nouwen chided him for belaboring the obvious. "Christianity is like marriage," he said to the speaker. "You can explain that you love Jesus the same way you love your wife."

"Yes, Henri," Colson replied, "but they can *see* my wife. They don't need me to convince them that she exists. But they do need reasons to believe that God exists."[3] Colson's point was that not seeing makes it hard to believe. Non-

Christians are hardly the only people who have this struggle. Sometimes Christians also have trouble loving a Savior they have never seen.

How God Keeps Us in His Love

The more we consider how hard it is to love Jesus sight unseen, the more remarkable it is to receive the affirmation Peter gives in the opening chapter of his first epistle. The apostle's voice rings out across the chasm of time and makes an astonishing statement about our relationship with Jesus: "Though you have not seen him, you love him" (1 Pet. 1:8). It would be amazing enough for Peter to claim that we *believe* in Jesus, which is something he also says: "Though you do not now see him, you believe in him" (v. 8). But first he speaks to the heart and says that we *love* Jesus—the Savior we have never seen.

As he wrote his letter, Peter was speaking to the global church of his own generation. Christianity had spread across the Roman world like a benevolent virus. One person shared the gospel with another person, who in turn shared it with someone else. This meant that most of the first recipients of Peter's letter were not eyewitnesses of the life, death, and resurrection of Jesus Christ. They had come to trust him later, either directly through the testimony of the apostles, or else indirectly through churches that the apostles planted.

This put the early Christians at something of a disadvantage. There was a difference between the way they knew Jesus and the way Peter knew him. As a disciple, Peter had seen it all: the Sermon on the Mount, the feeding of the five thousand, the Last Supper, Gethsemane, Calvary, and the gaping hole in the garden tomb. He loved what he saw, and loved Jesus because of it.

As Peter sat down to write a letter of encouragement to Christians across the Mediterranean, and as he reflected on their spiritual experience, he was amazed at their affection. The word "though" indicates the apostle's astonishment. These people had never seen Jesus. Nevertheless, they loved him—a fact that the Puritan Andrew Gray described as "a riddle, almost impossible to understand."[4]

More amazing still, Peter's correspondents loved Jesus even though their faith was being "tested by fire" (1 Pet. 1:7). At the opening of his letter, Peter acknowledges that his brothers and sisters were "grieved by various trials" (v. 6). They were going through a season of severe difficulty. Given what Peter later says about sharing Christ's sufferings, being insulted for Christ's name, and "suffering as a Christian" (4:12–19; cf. 5:8–10), this is almost certainly because they were being persecuted for the cause of Christ. In this context Peter says, "Though you have not seen him, you love him. Though you do not now see him, you believe in him and rejoice with joy that is inexpressible and filled with glory, obtaining the outcome of your faith, the salvation of your souls" (1:8–9).

Rather than causing them to walk away from Jesus, the

challenges that the early Christians faced were producing hope, joy, and the assurance of everlasting life. These people had a fire-tested faith. Most of all they had what the Puritan Thomas Vincent called *The True Christian's Love for the Unseen Christ*.[5]

Anyone who has ever been through fiery trials knows how hard it can be for faith to come through unscathed. Sometimes the grief that follows a death, the pain that goes with a broken relationship, the disappointment of not getting what we deserve, the discouragement of not achieving a goal that was desperately important to us, or the embarrassment that comes when people criticize our Christianity make it harder to trust in a Savior we have never seen.

So we need to ask: what enabled Peter's friends to keep believing without seeing? It was not what they did for themselves, but something God did for them. In the opening section of 1 Peter, the apostle praises God the Father for the blessings he gives through Jesus the Son by the power of the Holy Spirit. And all of the blessings Peter mentions are things that *God* does to keep us in the love of Jesus.

To review some of the main realities of our salvation, God caused us to be born again (1 Pet. 1:3), sending the Holy Spirit right inside us to give us new spiritual life. This means that we do not have to love Jesus with our own limited love; we can love him with the love that his loving Spirit pours into our hearts.

God also gave us a "living hope through the resurrection of Jesus Christ from the dead" (1 Pet. 1:3). Unless there is life after death, there is no ultimate hope for anyone. But on the third day, by the power of the Holy Spirit, God the Father raised Jesus the Son from the dead. We know this because Peter and the other disciples have given us multiple eyewitness accounts of their personal encounters with the risen Christ. So when we talk about the promise of eternal life, we are not just guessing. The true Word of God gives us solid hope for the life to come.

This is not all that God has done to keep us in love with Jesus. We are born again by his loving Spirit—something God did for us in the past. We are promised resurrection life in his gospel Word—something God will do for us in the future. We are also protected by his power, which is something he does for us in the present. "By God's power," Peter says, we "are being guarded through faith for a salvation ready to be revealed in the last time" (1 Pet. 1:5).

When trials come, God does not abandon us. He does not reject us and then expect us to keep on loving him even though he has long since stopped loving us. Instead, God is right here with us. He preserves and protects us, and therefore our love perseveres.

The Scottish Presbyterian theologian Thomas Boston compared the protection of God's love to the security that a baby has in a mother's arms.[6] Fortunately, this security does not depend on the baby! Sometimes babies hold on tightly, but many times they squirm and struggle to get away. A good mother never loses her grip, however; she holds her baby secure. Our loving Father does the same thing for us: he keeps us in his loving arms. Therefore, we do not fall away, but remain safe in his love.

How We "See" Jesus

As we consider what God has done, is doing, and will do for our salvation, it is important to notice how God's love is at work in our lives. We are born again by the Spirit. We have the hope of resurrection life. We are held safe by the power of God. These are the living realities of our faith. But do we see Jesus, and as we see him, do we love him more and more?

I use the word *see* deliberately. We cannot see him literally, of course. That is the main point of this passage, in which Peter marvels at our faith in the unseen Christ. But we can see Jesus metaphorically, and this reassures us in the reality of his love. So consider some of the places where we "see" Jesus.

We see Jesus every day in the beauty of his creation. Jesus Christ is the Creator God. Therefore, everything good in the world around us testifies to his wisdom and power. This should awaken within us a response of love for our Creator, who wants us to know him through his work. On the day I write these words, I am praising God for seeing a small flock of bay-breasted warblers descend on the lawn—a gift of beauty.

The glory of creation is one of the main things that

God used to bring Louis Zamperini to faith in Christ. Zamperini's remarkable story as an Olympic athlete, survivor at sea, prisoner of war, and Christian disciple is told in the best-selling biography *Unbroken*. In 1949 Zamperini attended Billy Graham's famous evangelistic crusades in Los Angeles. There he heard Dr. Graham ask why God allowed the world to suffer the ravages of war. The evangelist began his answer by saying,

> If you look into the heavens tonight, on this beautiful California night, I see the stars and can see the footprints of God. . . . I think to myself, my Father, my Heavenly Father, hung them there with a flaming fingertip and holds them there with the power of his omnipotent hand, and he runs the whole universe, and he's not too busy running the whole universe to count the hairs on my head and see a sparrow when it falls, because God is interested in me. . . . God spoke in creation.[7]

These words reminded Louis Zamperini of his encounter with God when he was lost at sea for forty-seven days during World War II, dying of thirst, drifting aimlessly in the doldrums on a tiny raft. One day he saw a beautiful sky reflected in the glassy sea. A leaping fish broke the surface, and suddenly Zamperini was filled with wondrous gratitude to a God he had never worshiped.

As the old soldier continued to listen, Billy Graham described God's invisibility as the truest test of faith. In order to know who "sees" him, God makes himself unseen. As he continued to listen, Louis felt God pressing in on him, and he wanted to flee. But as he headed for the exit, he remembered the rash promise he had made to God when his companions were dying of thirst and sharks were circling his raft: "If you will save me, I will serve you forever."[8] So instead of running away on the beautiful California night when he first heard the gospel, Louis Zamperini went forward and gave his life to the Savior he had seen first in creation. He went straight home, poured his liquor down the drain, and threw his pornography down the garbage chute. Once he had seen Jesus, he was never the same man again.

The next morning Louie Zamperini took his Bible to a nearby park, sat down under a tree, and began to read. This is another place where we see Jesus: in the pages of Scripture. The Bible is a love letter from home, in which our Savior tenders us his affections. When we read God's Word, we are not getting someone else on the other end of the line, but hearing the voice of God himself. So whenever we have trouble seeing Jesus, or find ourselves doubting the love of God, we should go back to the Bible.

Written words have the power to sustain a relationship between absent lovers. A remarkable example is the correspondence between Svetlana Ivanova and Lev Mishchenko, who was imprisoned in Stalin's Gulag. Over the course of eight years, Lev and Svetlana exchanged at least 1,246 letters. "We are both 29 years old," Svetlana wrote in one of them:

We first met 11 years ago, and we haven't seen each other for 5 years. It is terrible to spell out these figures, but time passes, Lev. And I know you will do all you can so that we can meet before another five years pass. I'm becoming stubborn, Lev. How many times have I wanted to nestle in your arms, but could only turn to the empty wall in front of me? I felt I couldn't breathe. Yet time would pass, and I would pull myself together. We will get through this, Lev.[9]

Eventually, Lev and Svetlana were reunited. Their love survived, and what enabled its survival was the written word. "The point of all this," Svetlana wrote in another letter, "is that I want to tell you just three words—two of them are pronouns and the third is a verb (to be read in all the tenses simultaneously: past, present and future)."

Jesus has written the same three words to us in the Bible. "I love you," he says, over and over and over again. "I have loved you, I do love you, and I will love you." We see Jesus in the love promises of his Word.

Another place we see the love of Jesus is in the sacraments. The sacred rites of baptism and Communion are visible words that speak to us of his saving love. Although we cannot see Jesus hanging on the cross, he has given us signs and seals of his grace. In baptism, we see the cleansing power of Christ's purifying sacrifice. In Communion (or, the Eucharist), we see his body broken and his blood spilled for our sins—not literally, but figuratively. Baptism and the Lord's Supper are God's way of saying, "See, this is how real my grace is for you—as real as this water, this bread, and this cup." The unseen Christ has given us something to smell, touch, and taste, and this is a confirmation of his affection.

Jesus also gives us one another. The church is a visible witness to his love. "No one has ever seen God," the Scripture says, but "if we love one another, God abides in us and his love is perfected in us" (1 John 4:12). This is one of the reasons it is so important for us to grow in love. The way we care for one another is meant to show people the love of a Savior they have never seen. An old chorus from the 1970s goes like this: "They will know we are Christians by our love." The chorus expresses one biblical truth. But here is another biblical truth: "They will know he is Jesus by our love." The love people see in us helps them receive the love of the unseen Christ.

When We Finally See Him

The more we "see" Jesus—in creation, in Scripture, in the sacraments, and in the church—the more we will grow to love him. In fact, once we truly see him, it is impossible for us *not* to love him, and also to long for the day when we will finally see him face to face.

The challenge that Peter identified in his epistle—of loving an unseen Savior—is not permanent, but temporary. A day is coming when our faith will become sight. The apostle emphasizes the certainty of this promise by saying that our inheritance is "imperishable, undefiled, unfading" (1 Pet. 1:4). God is keeping salvation secure for us in heaven. It is "ready to be revealed," Peter says (v. 5). Soon there will be "praise and glory and honor at the revelation of Jesus Christ" (v. 7). When the apostle says "revelation," he is talking about something we can't see now but will see then: the visible appearance of Jesus. One day we will see the unseen Christ.

The certainty of this promise helps to explain the joy we experience in the Christian life, even when we are going through trials. We live in the hope of seeing Jesus. To return to the main text for this chapter and to quote Peter again: "Though you do not now see him, you believe in him and rejoice with joy that is inexpressible and filled with glory, obtaining the outcome of your faith, the salvation of your souls" (1 Pet. 1:8–9).

People sometimes say, "Seeing is believing." The biblical perspective is almost the opposite. For the followers of Christ, believing is seeing! If we believe, then one day we will see. Like Peter, we will be eyewitness of the risen Christ. We will see Jesus with our own two eyes.

Here is how Thomas Boston described the sight that will greet believers at the resurrection of the dead:

> They shall see Jesus Christ, God and man, with their bodily eyes, as He will never lay aside the human nature. They will behold that glorious blessed body, which is personally united to the divine nature, and

exalted above principalities and powers and every name that is named. There we shall see, with our eyes, that very body which was born of Mary at Bethlehem, and crucified at Jerusalem between two thieves: the blessed head that was crowned with thorns; the face that was spit upon; the hands and feet that were nailed to the cross; all shining with inconceivable glory. The glory of the man Christ will attract the eyes of all the saints.[10]

This glorious vision is the hope of every believer in Jesus, of every true lover of the unseen Christ. A notable example comes from the last earthly moments of the Christian hymn writer Frances Havergal. When Havergal was lying on her deathbed, it appeared to her family members that she was catching her first glimpse of her beautiful Savior. In describing the scene, her sister Maria wrote:

And now she looked up steadfastly as if she saw the Lord. . . . For ten minutes we watched that almost visible meeting with her King, and her countenance was so glad, as if she were already talking to him. Then she tried to sing, but after one sweet high note, "He . . ." her voice failed, and she passed away.[11]

What Havergal saw in those moments is something every living believer is waiting to see—a mystery of the unseen Christ. If we believe, one day we will see!

Loving Jesus Perfectly

The story of William Montague Dyke is almost too good to be true. As the story goes, William was blinded in an accident at age ten. Despite his disability, he went on to graduate from university with high honors. During his student days he fell in love with the daughter of a high-ranking British naval officer and they were engaged to be married.

Shortly before the wedding, William had experimental eye surgery in the hope that his sight would be restored. If the surgery failed, he would remain blind for the rest of his life. But there was a possibility it would succeed, in which case William—a true romantic—wanted the face of his fair bride to be the first vision that filled his gaze. So he insisted on keeping the bandages over his eyes until the wedding.

When the happy day arrived, many guests assembled to witness the exchange of vows: cabinet members, courtiers, even royalty. The groom stood at the front of the church with his father and the doctor who had performed the surgery. The triumphant strains of the organ filled the sanctuary as the bride walked majestically down the aisle. When she arrived at the altar, the surgeon took a pair of scissors and carefully cut the bandages from William's eyes.

The tension in the room was almost unbearable. Witnesses held their breath as they waited to learn what, if anything, the groom was able to see. As he stood face to face with his bride, William Montague Dyke gasped, "You are more beautiful than I ever imagined!"[1]

Love Story

As I said, this story is almost too good to be true. I was suspicious enough to do a little research and discovered that although William Montague Dyke was a real person— a descendant of Charlemagne the Great and the second son of the 7th Baronet of Horeham—he died in infancy. Thus William never reached his tenth birthday, let alone went to university or married the daughter of a naval officer.

Nonetheless, this apocryphal story points to a gospel truth: one day we will see Jesus face to face. At present, as lovers of the unseen Christ, we worship an invisible Savior. But a day is coming when our faith will become sight. And if we love Jesus now—sight unseen—we can scarcely imagine what joy will be ours at his glorious revelation.

The Bible uses matrimonial imagery to describe that awesome day (e.g., Rev. 19:9). A match has been made in heaven between the noblest of all grooms—the Son of God—and his beautiful bride, the church. When our wedding day finally arrives, the bandages will come off, we will see Jesus face to face, and we will truly say what William Montague Dyke supposedly said to his beloved: "You are more beautiful than I ever imagined!"

According to Scripture, our relationship with Jesus is a romance. So in Ephesians 5—where Paul describes the ideal marriage, in which a wife honors her husband with loving submission and a husband gives himself up for his wife with loving sacrifice—the apostle says that in addressing marriage he is really talking about the mysterious matrimony between Christ and the church. Every believer is betrothed to Jesus.

As we get ready for our wedding day—as we prepare to celebrate the everlasting nuptials—our love for Jesus grows (or at least it ought to). After all, when a bride and groom are truly and deeply in love, they look forward to their wedding day with joyful expectation. Their anticipation grows every day, and so does their love.

It is not surprising, then, that when the Bible talks about the second coming of Jesus Christ, it uses the vocabulary of love. For example, when the apostle Paul came to the end of his life, he said, "Henceforth there is laid up for me the crown of righteousness, which the Lord, the righteous judge, will award to me on that Day, and not only to me but also to all who have *loved* his appearing" (2 Tim. 4:8). We anticipate the sudden appearance of

Jesus Christ—his visible return—with affectionate devotion. "Keep yourselves in the love of God," Jude tells us, "waiting for the mercy of our Lord Jesus Christ that leads to eternal life" (Jude 21).

These and other passages tell us something important about eternal life: the people who are destined to see Jesus in the life to come are in love with him already. This makes perfect sense. Why would we even *want* to be with Jesus, unless we loved him? But if we do love him, this is a sign that we are destined to belong to him forever—to "receive the crown of life, which God has promised to those who love him" (James 1:12). Eternal life is for lovers who long to see Jesus after a long time apart.

Thinking about absent lovers reminds me how badly I wanted to see Lisa Maxwell in the summer of 1985. We had fallen in love during our freshman year at Wheaton College (or rather, I had fallen in love, and then spent almost half a year trying to convince her that she should try falling in love, too). As soon as the school year ended, Lisa headed to northern Wisconsin to teach canoeing and sailing at Honey Rock Camp. I handled the separation badly. Time alone tempted me to wonder whether I really wanted to stay in the relationship. Rather than keeping this to myself until I worked things out, I told Lisa how uncertain I was feeling—a selfish betrayal that wounded a trusting heart.

Thank God, it did not take me long to regain my sanity. By the time I could get off work for a few days, I was desperate to see her, and to say in person the only two words that needed to be said. I got in the car after work on a Friday night, strapped a dozen roses into the passenger seat, and headed north. Lisa still didn't know where things stood between us, or what I would say when I got there. The closer I got to Honey Rock, the faster I drove, assuming that unincorporated towns in northern Wisconsin did not have police officers (they do, actually, but that's a different story). I was desperate to see the love of my life.

When I got to Honey Rock, all it took was one look between us for her to know that I was sorry and for me to know that I was forgiven. This is because we were truly in love: the love we shared when we were reunited was already there.

My point in sharing this personal narrative is simply to say that we feel the same way about Jesus. We want to see him because we love him. Our expectation for his coming is the desperate longing of a devoted lover.

Not Yet

Admittedly, we do not love Jesus as well as we should or as much as we will. This is something we have tried to be honest about in this book: there are times when we don't love Jesus. And even when we do, it is hard for us to stay in love. When we hear Jesus warn about people forsaking their first love (Rev. 2:4; cf. Matt. 24:12), or hear Paul say that anyone who does not love the Lord will be cursed (1 Cor. 16:22), we fear that this could happen to us. So we need to hold on to the remarkable hope that Paul offers in a blessing from the end of his letter to the Ephesians: "Peace be to the brothers, and love with faith, from God the Father and the Lord Jesus Christ. Grace be with all who love our Lord Jesus Christ with love incorruptible" (Eph. 6:23–24).

"Love incorruptible." This phrase is a conundrum for the commentators. Literally, the verse reads, "Grace be with all who love our Lord Jesus in incorruption." So "incorruptible" is a fair translation. But what does this mean, and how is it possible?

Some scholars have tried to connect the incorruptible love at the end of the verse back to the grace at the beginning and make it God's love.[2] After all, only his love is truly incorruptible; our own affection is feeble and fickle. But on this reading the God of all grace promises to love us with a perfect love. This is shown supremely in his death on the cross for our sins and his resurrection from the grave. That is just the beginning of his affection, however. God has promised to love us to the end; nothing can ever separate us from the love of Jesus Christ our Lord (see Rom. 8:35–39). He will love us "in incorruption," meaning that his imperishable love will last into eternity.

This way of looking at Ephesians 6:24 is theologically sound, but syntactically improbable. As a result, most commentators see "love incorruptible" as referring to us rather than to God. Who will receive God's grace? People who love Jesus with unfailing, undying affection.

But this raises a further question, which for most of us is more like a worry. How can my love ever meet this standard? How can I say in good conscience that I love Jesus with an immortal, incorruptible love?

Our goal in this book has been to grow in our love for Jesus. As we continue in the Christian life, we want our affections to increase, so that we have a greater heart for our Savior. The question is, are we making any progress? Do we love Jesus more now than we did when we began trying to grow in our affection for him?

I have quoted several times from a Puritan classic by Thomas Vincent, *The True Christian's Love for the Unseen Christ*. Vincent gave his book a long subtitle, which most Christians probably can relate to: *A Discourse, Chiefly Tending to Excite and Promote the Decaying Love of Christ in the Hearts of Christians*. Sometimes we love Jesus more, but then again, sometimes we love him less. Our hearts are susceptible to spiritual decay.

If we doubt this, all we need to do is to consider some of the searching questions that Thomas Vincent uses to expose a lack of love in the believer's heart:

> Does not the little zeal which you have for Christ's honor in the world argue that you have but little love to him? Where is your activity for Christ to promote His interest among those relations and friends that you

have acquaintance with? Do you labor all you can to bring others into the ways of God and into acquaintance with Christ? Besides, will not your little secret devotion argue your little affection unto Christ? Will not your closets, or other retiring places, witness how little you are in secret prayer and converse with Christ there? Brief and straitened prayer in secret argues a heart straitened in love to Jesus Christ.[3]

If we are compelled to admit that loving Jesus more is a struggle for us, then we are likely to read the blessing at the end of Ephesians with a certain amount of ambivalence. Does God have grace for me, or not? The grace he offers is for "all who love our Lord Jesus Christ with love incorruptible" (Eph. 6:24). But loving Jesus is exactly my weakness. So what blessing does he have for me?

Various Bible scholars translate the end of this verse in different ways. Some take the phrase "in incorruption" temporally, as a reference to eternity, in which case God's grace is for people who love Jesus forever—an immortal love that begins already in this life. Others take it morally, as a reference to the purity of a person's love. To love Jesus "in incorruption," then, is to love him with perfect sincerity.

No matter which definition we choose, however, we all fail to meet God's standard. If we love Jesus at all, it is not with an incorruptible love, but with some lesser affection. So when we read Ephesians 6:24, it may be tempting to think that we are outside of the grace of God.

There are several ways to resolve this difficulty. One is to say that the Bible is not, in fact, demanding perfection. After all, this verse begins with grace, which is always for people who *fail* to meet God's standard—for sinners in need of salvation. So when we get to the end of the verse, where Paul talks about incorruptible love, we may safely assume he means love that is generally sincere, but not absolutely perfect, because perfection would be impossible for anyone.

We can take this interpretation one step further by observing that one day we *will* love Jesus perfectly. This verse may be looking forward in hope. Whether we define its love as unfailing, undying, or incorruptible, a day is coming when we will love Jesus with everything we have—with all our mind, heart, soul, and strength. Although it will not happen in this life, it will happen in the life to come. So the grace that God offers in Ephesians 6:24 really *is* for us—not because we are perfect lovers yet, but because we will be when Jesus comes again.

Immortal Beloved

For us to reach this goal, a miraculous transformation must take place—what theologians call "glorification." In order for us to love Jesus with an incorruptible love, we have to be totally delivered from sin and made completely holy.

William Cowper hoped to reach perfect sanctification all his life. The English poet, who was famous for his translations of Homer and for hymns like "God Moves in a Mysterious Way," struggled with depression throughout adulthood. He suffered at least four mental breakdowns and repeatedly attempted suicide. For three years in his thirties Cowper was institutionalized for insanity. A decade later, when he was at the height of his career, he believed that he was destined for damnation and that therefore God was commanding him to kill himself—a lie straight from hell.

Yet even in the desperate suffering of his dark soul, William Cowper was guarded by the grace of God. One of his hymns expresses the poet's longing for a greater love. The hymn begins with a question:

Hark, my soul, it is the Lord;
'Tis thy Savior, hear His Word;
Jesus speaks, and speaks to thee,
"Say, poor sinner, lovest thou me?"

This is a question that every poor sinner has to answer: do I love Jesus, or not? In the hymn Cowper encourages his soul by imagining his Savior testifying to his own unchanging love—a saving love that is "free and faithful, strong as death." But eventually the question returns, and the hymn writer has to answer for himself: does he love Jesus, or not?

As he examines his heart, Cowper has to confess that he is a man of inconstant affections. So he ends his hymn with a prayer for the kind of grace that God offers in Ephesians 6:

> Lord, it is my chief complaint,
> That my love is weak and faint;
> Yet I love Thee, and adore:
> Oh for grace to love thee more!

Thomas Cranmer composed a similar prayer when he first wrote the *Book of Common Prayer*:

Almightie God, unto whom all hartes bee open, and all desires knowen, and from whom no secretes are hid: clense the thoughts of our hartes, by the inspiracion of thy holy spirite: that we may perfectly love thee, and worthily magnifie thy holy name: through Christ our Lord. Amen.[4]

One day this holy prayer will be answered—not just for William Cowper and Thomas Cranmer, but for everyone who wants to love Jesus more. Our entrance into God's presence will be the perfection of our affection. Our hearts will be all for Jesus, only for Jesus, forever.

It is hard for us even to imagine what it will be like to love with a divine and perfect love. In this life we always seem to be loving the wrong things too much and the right things too little. But a day of perfect love is coming: "What no eye has seen, nor ear heard, nor the heart of man imagined, what God has prepared for those who love him" (1 Cor. 2:9).

Augustine had a marvelous way of expressing the perfection of our affection. The great North African theologian of the fourth and fifth centuries observed that in their creation, Adam and Eve were able to sin *or* not to sin. Sadly, their first disobedience subjected our entire race to the bondage of sin. Now we are not able *not* to sin. But Augustine believed that one day we will receive even greater grace than our first parents received. In the kingdom to come, we will not be able to sin![5]

Heaven's perfection will transform our hearts. We will not just love Jesus more; we will love him the most—as much as we possibly can. We will have a superlative, joyful affection for our everlasting Savior. To follow the sanctified logic of Thomas Vincent, "If the joy of a Christian, while he is here below, is unspeakable and full of glory, what joy must the saints that are now made perfect have, in the immediate contemplation of Jesus Christ?"[6]

None of us has yet lived with this kind of love. So how can we describe it? Thomas Vincent used several adjectives to describe the love that we ought to have—and one day will have by the grace of God—for Jesus. He said our love for Jesus should be marked by sincerity, supremacy, ardency, and constancy.[7]

Our love for Jesus will be *sincere*. We will not merely pretend to love Jesus, but we will actually love him. Whatever outward actions may give people the impression that we love Jesus will be fully matched by our inward affections.

Our love for Jesus will be *supreme*. The human heart only has room for one dominating love. In this life, many loves lay claim to our hearts. But when Jesus comes, we will love him most of all, and this will order all of our other affections.

Our love for Jesus will be *ardent*. That is to say, our love will be heartfelt. As we gaze upon our Savior's face, giving him all our praise and worship, our hearts will burn within us in a blaze of pure spiritual affection.

Our love for Jesus will be *constant*. Now our love is more like daisy petals: I love him, I love him not. But in the life to come, our love will burn as an eternal flame, always shining bright for our Savior, never diminished, never extinguished.

Staying in Love

Sincerity, supremacy, ardency, constancy—such perfection will stay beyond our reach for the rest of our earthly lives. But if we love Jesus at all, we will keep striving for incorruptible affection, wanting to love him more and more.

One way to nurture our love for Jesus is by spending time with him alone. Lovers always find time to be with the one they love. Where is the place—and when is the time—when you will go to meet with Jesus? Thomas Vincent had this advice for people who want to experience more love for the unseen Christ:

> Spend time in secret retirement, and there think and think again of the superlative excellencies and perfections which are in Christ's person; how wonderful

and matchless His love is, what heights that cannot be reached, what depths in it that cannot be fathomed, what other dimensions which cannot be comprehended. Meditate often on His benefits, how incomparable His love is; and, while you are looking, you feel your hearts leaping. . . . O the ravishments of love! The transports of soul which some believers have found in their retired thoughts and views of Christ![8]

It is hard to imagine, but one day we will love Jesus with all the love our hearts can bear. In the meantime, we grow in love as we meditate on the Father's love for us in the Son—the love that led him to the cross, rescued us from sin, and brought us back from death to spiritual life—the wide, long, high, deep love of Jesus—the love that goes beyond human knowing.

The true story of Lap Vi Ho illustrates how important it is to keep love alive. In the days leading up to the fall of Saigon, Lap was desperate to get his family to safety. This was in January of 1975, when the Americans were pulling out of South Vietnam. As a senior administrator at the University of Saigon, Lap feared for his life. Fortunately, he was able to send his pregnant wife and young son ahead to Bangkok, Thailand. But when he showed up at the airport a few days later, planning to join them, his passport was confiscated and he was thrown in prison.

Over the next five years Lap Vi Ho did everything humanly possible to rejoin his family. He escaped and was recaptured six times, only to suffer extreme hardship, deprivation, and abuse afterward. The seventh time proved to be the charm, however. Lap escaped from camp and walked to Cambodia, where he was promptly captured by the vicious army of the Khmer Rouge. Remarkably, he escaped again, and helped thirty other prisoners commandeer a boat and row all the way to Thailand, where he was taken to a camp for refugees.

In the meantime, Lap Vi Ho's wife had given birth to their daughter. She wanted her children to grow up loving their father, so she would show them his picture every day, talking about him and praying for him. It is strange to say, but the little girl grew up without ever saying a word. She seemed to be fully intelligent, yet for some reason—maybe it was sadness—she was unable or unwilling to speak.

Then came the day of their happy reunion. Word of Lap's escape reached his wife and children. They quickly traveled to his refugee camp, and when they arrived, Lap's daughter recognized her father immediately. She ran to him, fell into his arms, and began to talk excitedly. Her parents say that she hasn't stopped talking since![9]

One day we will see Jesus for the very first time. We will recognize him right away, because we spend time with him every day, hearing about him in God's Word and seeing his picture in the gospel. Though we have not seen him, we love him. And when we finally do see him, we will fall into his arms, tell him our praises, and never stop.

Study Guide

by Nancy Ryken Taylor

Chapter 1: Where Love Comes From

Sometimes we approach our relationship with God more as a to-do list than a friendship. We know we should love God more, and may even want to do so, but we go about it all wrong. We want a ten-step list guaranteed to increase our love for God. Or else we want to do something for him rather than simply being with him and letting his love saturate our hearts so we can return that love to him. Sadly, our efforts often miss the point and we are left feeling cold. The good news is that there is a better way.

1. The Bible portrays God's relationship with his people as a spiritual marriage between a perfectly loving groom and an unfaithful wife. What does this image tell us about God's love for us? What are some adjectives that describe the love a husband ought to have for his wife?

2. Why is it so easy for us to fall out of love with God
   when he does so much for us? What factors make us
   fickle in our affection for him?

3. At what moments in life were you most in love with
   Jesus? What circumstances contributed to that "head-
   over-heels" feeling? What were the results of your
   overflowing love—what behaviors or attitudes were
   different at those times than at times when you have
   felt distant from God?

4. Read Romans 5:1–5 and notice the ultimate source of
   love. What implications does this truth have for our
   lives? How does it make us live and love differently
   to know that our love comes from God through the
   Holy Spirit?

5. Jonathan Edwards said that the Spirit's office is "to
   communicate divine love to the Creature."[1] Read Ga-
   latians 5:16, 25 and 1 Thessalonians 5:19. What is our
   role in opening ourselves to the Holy Spirit's work in
   our lives? How can we invite the third person of the
   Trinity to communicate God's love to us?

6. What are some ways that you have grieved or quenched
   the Holy Spirit? Take time to repent of those sins.

7. What do you hope to get out of your study of this
   book? What is one way you hope to grow in your love
   for Jesus?

Chapter 2: This I Know

No one wants to experience times of doubt, and yet we all
do. The key is to find a way to focus on what we know to

be true so that our doubts become a catalyst for growth in our love for God rather than a cause for despondency. When we finally come out on the other side of doubt with a more confident faith, we may be more in love than ever with the God who is true, dependable, and unchanging—the God who in his mercy responds to all our doubts with love and faithfulness.

1. Do you find spiritual doubts to be more like ants (a useful agitation), mosquitoes (just plain irritating), or some other insect? How can doubt help grow your faith? What can you do to make doubt an impetus for positive change rather than a catalyst for disbelief and despair?

2. Do your doubts more resemble those of Asaph (Psalm 73), David (Psalms 13; 22; etc.), or the desperate father in Mark 9? To put it another way, what is the usual cause of your doubt—injustice and inequality in life, spiritual depression, the attacks of enemies, the difficulties of life, or something else?

3. What weapons should be used to fight these causes of doubt? Do the strategies necessary to fight each kind of doubt differ, and if so, how?

4. Read Titus 3:3–8, the before-and-after picture of life without and life with the gospel. What marks the turning point between a life of doubt and evil and a life of hope and goodness? Who initiates the change, and how is it accomplished?

5. What Bible passage(s) do you find especially helpful when you are experiencing times of doubt or spiritual

discouragement? What story or verse do you go back to again and again for the reassurance of God's love?

6. Other than turning to Scripture, what other strategies might help a friend who is experiencing spiritual doubt?

7. List some of the blessings that God has poured out on you—both spiritual realities as expressed in Scripture and the blessings he has provided in your life on earth. As you make your list, marvel at God's love for you and return to him your praise.

Chapter 3: With All We Have

When we are engrossed in reading a book or working on a project, it is easy for us to focus all our energy on the task at hand and tune out the world around us. We may even forget to eat if we are fully captivated by what we're learning. When we dedicate our minds to loving God, we can apply the same type of energy and hyperfocus to our learning and worship. In this way, we take every thought captive in obedience to Christ (2 Cor. 10:5).

1. John Piper explains the connection between thought and emotion like this: "Right thinking about God exists to serve right feelings for God."[2] Discuss a time in your life when right thinking led to right feelings.

2. What are some practical ways to love God with all of our minds? As you desire to deepen your relationship with God, what is one thing you would like to try in the coming week?

3. In what ways do you think and study differently because you are a Christian? How does your relationship with Christ affect your intellectual life? How can the study of biology, history, philosophy, or other subjects help you to love God more? How can you engage your mind in such a way that even secular study comes under the lordship of Christ?

4. In his book *Think*, John Piper writes, "The main reason God has given us minds is that we might seek out and find all the reasons that exist for treasuring him *in* all things and *above* all things."[3] How do your own intellectual pursuits enhance your love for God? How could you use your mind to better enhance your treasuring of him?

5. What role does the life of the mind play in evangelism? In extending compassion to others?

6. There are, of course, limits to study. Read 1 Corinthians 1:20–31 and 2:7–8. What are the differences between human wisdom and divine wisdom? What must people who wish to be truly wise embrace in order to be saved?

7. What are the pitfalls or limits of earthly wisdom? In what ways can knowledge lead us away from God? How can we safeguard against this danger?

Chapter 4: What Makes Love Extravagant

It is easy for us to go about daily life without giving much thought to how much we have been forgiven by God. We look at our own sins and think of them as relatively insignificant or easily justified, whereas the sins of others may seem larger than life. But at those rare moments when we come face-to-face with the depth of our depravity, if we know God's mercy for us in Jesus, we can be overwhelmed with love. This is what happened to the sinful woman in Luke 7.

1. In your interactions with other people, how have you seen forgiveness foster love?

2. Read Luke 7:36–50. To some, the woman's extravagant expression of love might have seemed improper. Have you ever been so overwhelmed with God's grace that you responded with an extravagant expression of love? What obstacles stand in the way of worshiping God more freely?

3. What words would you use to describe the sinful woman? Think both of her external circumstances and of her internal attitudes. How would you describe Simon the Pharisee? How would you summarize the fundamental spiritual difference between the two?

4. What can you tell about Jesus from this story—about his character and identity? What details in this story should cause us to fall on our knees in worship?

5. What people or circumstances tempt you to resemble Simon the Pharisee in his smug judgmentalism? When confronted with people you view as particularly sinful, are you more of a lover or more of a critic? What can you do to increase your compassion and decrease your condemnation?

6. Discuss the questions raised in this chapter: What would happen if we really believed that God has grace for sinners—not just for us, but for everyone? What would happen if we embraced lost and difficult people instead of avoiding them? What would happen in their lives, and what would happen in our lives?

7. Name one thing you plan to do this week to express more extravagant love to God.

Chapter 5: What Love Does

Once you have been overwhelmed by God's love for you, a desire to love him back will follow naturally. But sometimes it is hard to know what we can do to show our love to him. What can we offer to the almighty God who created us and gave everything to us? In a word, we can offer obedience—obedience not from a sense of duty or an attempt to earn God's love, but as a willing response to the love that belongs to us in Jesus.

1. On a day-to-day basis, how do you show God that you love him? How do those actions change when you are experiencing times of discouragement or doubt?

2. Read John 14:15–27. How does God want us to show our love for him? How are we able to do this?

3. Habitual sin is usually an indication that we do not understand or appropriate some aspect of God's love or the reality of who we are in Christ. What can we do to clarify such misunderstandings? How can we make

our obedience more a response to God's love and less a duty?

4. Where does contemporary culture misunderstand the relationship between love and obedience to God's law, or between mercy and justice? What are some practical ways we can help people understand the Bible's perspective on how these seeming opposites fit together?

5. How can you show more love this week to the people you live with? How can you do a better job of loving people in your church? Of loving your neighbors? Make some specific plans and goals.

6. In what areas of life do you sense that you are not being completely obedient to God's laws? What habits or attitudes do you wish to change with the help of the Holy Spirit? Share these with someone who can help encourage you to pursue the changes you desire.

Chapter 6: Love's Greatest Test

It doesn't take long to discover that the church is made up of very imperfect people. Indeed, some of our deepest wounds come from people in the body of Christ. It may even seem as if life would be simpler and less painful outside of the church. But these hurts do not excuse us from investing in the lives of fellow believers in a local church. Allowing the Bible to set our expectations of and commitments to the body of Christ is a good first step toward healthier and happier relationships with other Christians.

1. Some Christians seem to approach the church as consumers. How have you seen this to be true? When have you been tempted to treat church that way?

2. How do people outside the church (nonbelievers) judge the sincerity of a Christian's faith? What are some criteria by which Christians are judged by other believers? How fair or unfair are these standards?

3. Why is it sometimes harder to love people inside the church than people outside the church? What can we do to overcome the challenges of loving our brothers and sisters, particularly those who are hard to love?

4. Do you often think of loving God's people, the church, as a way to show God that you love him, or was this a new idea for you? In what ways should your relationship with the church resemble a romance?

5. Read Hebrews 10:25 and Ephesians 3:10–11; 4:1–13; 5:22–29. Why should a Christian be involved in a local church? How would you counsel new believers about how to participate in an imperfect church? How should they handle the inevitable disagreements and disappointments?

6. If we are trying to approach the church as lovers rather than consumers, what types of disagreements or annoyances within the church should we tolerate? How can a believer know when the time has come to find a new church home?

7. Are you satisfied with your attitude toward your church? If not, what are some ways that you would like to grow in your love for God's people?

Chapter 7: When I Don't Love Jesus

St. John of the Cross called it the "dark night of the soul." Martyn Lloyd-Jones termed it "spiritual depression." Keith Green described it in a song: "My eyes are dry, my faith is old. My heart is hard, my prayers are cold."[4] However we define it, we all have times when God feels distant and our love for him grows cold; this is a normal part of the Christian life. But what should we do about it?

1. In chapter 2 we saw some ways that doubt can spur us on toward deeper faith and greater love for Jesus. How can times of spiritual dryness or coldheartedness, when we simply do not feel much love for God, be good for our faith?

2. Read Mark 10:17–31. Have you ever had a conversation with someone who thought he or she could earn a way to heaven through personal effort? How did you respond? After reading this chapter, would your response be any different?

3. The rich young ruler thought he was self-sufficient, that he could earn his way to heaven through good deeds or buy security with his wealth. What things are you tempted to rely on to make it through life rather than trusting God? What ability or accomplishment makes you feel proud or self-righteous?

4. Imagine having a conversation with Jesus like the rich young ruler did. What do you think Jesus would tell *you* to give up for the kingdom of God? (See 2 Tim.

3:2–4 for a helpful list of common idols.) What is the "darling sin" you love more than Jesus?

5. Consider Peter's remark to Jesus in Mark 10:28. We might expect Jesus to tell Peter to be more humble. How does Jesus respond instead? Why do you think Jesus responded as he did?

6. In the story at the end of this chapter, a minister told a little girl who said she didn't love Jesus to go home and say, "Jesus loves me, Jesus loves me." What have you done when your affections felt cold that has reignited your love for Christ?

Chapter 8: Sight Unseen

One thing that sets Christians apart from the rest of the world is that we admit to believing things on faith that we cannot see with our eyes. Nonbelievers do the same thing, of course. C. S. Lewis famously pointed out that everyone has faith that the sun will rise again tomorrow. But believers base their lives on a God they can't see physically—and they receive untold spiritual riches when they do so.

1. Describe a time when you were skeptical about something, but then came to believe it. What caused you to move from doubt to faith?

2. Although faith rests on what is unseen, there are many proofs that the Bible is a reliable source of truth. What evidence of God's existence or the historicity of Jesus's death and resurrection is most convincing to you?

3. Read 1 Peter 1:3–9. What caused these new believers to rejoice? What obstacles to faith did they face?

4. In what ways do you identify with the joys and trials of the first Christians? What in Peter's description of their experiences of faith has not been part of your experience?

5. According to 1 Peter 1:3–9, what is God doing for us? What effect should this have on our faith?

6. We can't see or touch God physically, but how do you see him and feel his touch metaphorically in ways that strengthen your faith?

7. Describe a time when you have seen faith shine through during times of difficulty, either in your own life or in the life of someone you admire.

Chapter 9: Loving Jesus Perfectly

As we come to the end of this book, we find comfort in knowing that love ultimately comes from God, and that he will perfect our love as we trust in him. Enjoy this time of reflection on lessons learned with anticipation of the great joy that awaits us in heaven, where we will love Jesus perfectly.

1. Have you ever thought of life in heaven as a joyous reunion "for lovers who long to see Jesus after a long time apart"? What would be different about your actions and attitudes today if you truly felt this way?

2. Read Paul's instructions to young Timothy in 1 Timothy 4:5–8. Why did Paul look forward to Christ's appear-

ing? To what degree do you share his eager anticipation of that day, and why?

3. Read Revelation 2:2–5. What were the Ephesians doing well? What was the main problem with their church, and what threefold solution is offered?

4. Which of Thomas Vincent's characteristics of love for God—sincerity, supremacy, ardency, or constancy—comes most naturally to you? Which one is most difficult? Why?

5. Where is the place and when is the time you go to meet with Jesus? If you are not consistent in this area, what simple plan or next step would you like to implement to nurture your time and space with him?

6. What is the overarching life lesson you will take away from reading this book? What truth from these pages will help you love Jesus more?

Notes

Chapter 1: Where Love Comes From

1. Thomas Vincent, *The True Christian's Love to the Unseen Christ* (Ligonier, PA: Soli Deo Gloria, 1996), 2.
2. A. W. Tozer, *The Knowledge of the Holy* (New York: Harper Brothers, 1961), 105.
3. Ibid.
4. Jerry Trousdale, *Miraculous Movements: How Hundreds of Thousands of Muslims Are Falling in Love with Jesus* (Nashville, TN: Thomas Nelson, 2012), 26–31.
5. Vincent, *True Christian's Love to the Unseen Christ*, 31.
6. Jonathan Edwards, *Jonathan Edwards: Representative Selections, with Introduction, Bibliography, and Notes*, rev. ed., ed. C. H. Faust and T. H. Johnson, American Century series (New York: Hill and Wang, 1962), 378.
7. Timothy Dudley-Smith, "Safe in the Shadow of the Lord," 1970.
8. John R. W. Stott used this quotation in his last public address, entitled "The Model—Becoming More Like Christ," at Keswick, UK, July 17, 2007.
9. For a first-person account, see Trousdale, *Miraculous Movements*, 78–79.

Chapter 2: This I Know

1. Elizabeth Payson Prentiss, quoted in Robert J. Morgan, *Then Sings My Soul: 150 of the World's Greatest Hymn Stories* (Nashville, TN: Thomas Nelson, 2003), 133.

2. Frederick Buechner, *Wishful Thinking: A Theological ABC* (Harper & Row: New York, 1973), 21.

3. Roger White, *One Bird, One Cage, One Flight: Homage to Emily Dickinson* (Happy Camp, CA: Naturegraph, 1983), 52.

4. John Updike, *In the Beauty of the Lilies* (New York: Knopf, 1996), 5–6.

5. See George W. Knight III, *The Pastoral Epistles*, The New International Greek Testament Commentary (Grand Rapids, MI: Eerdmans, 1992), 339.

6. "Hark the Herald Angels Sing" (1739); "O Come, All Ye Faithful" (1751); "See, amid the Winter's Snow" (1851).

7. A version of these frequently quoted words appears on page 442 of the April 1896 issue of *The Homiletic Review*.

8. David McHale, from a 2012 ministry letter for His Mansion Ministries; shared with permission.

9. Prentiss, quoted in Morgan, *Then Sings My Soul*, 133.

10. Ibid.

Chapter 3: With All We Have

1. A. W. Tozer, *The Divine Conquest* (New York, NY: Fleming H. Revell, 1950), 101.

2. John Piper and D. A. Carson, *The Pastor as Scholar and the Scholar as Pastor: Reflections on Life and Ministry* (Wheaton, IL: Crossway, 2011), 50.

3. James C. Wilhoit and Evan B. Howard, *Discovering Lectio Divina: Bringing Scripture into Ordinary Life* (Downers Grove, IL: InterVarsity, 2012), 61.

4. Søren Kierkegaard, quoted in Wilhoit and Howard, *Discovering Lectio Divina*, 32.

5. Francis Schaeffer, quoted in *Creation Care*, April 2012, 22.

6. Rose Binney Salter's testimony was originally documented by Stephen West in "Conversion of an African Woman," *The Theological Magazine, or Synopsis of Modern Religious Sentiment on a New Plan*, vol. 2, no. 3 (1797): 194.

7. Ibid.

8. John Calvin Webster, "The Address," *Voice of Our Young People*, vol. 1, no. 3 (1868): 2–3.
9. Thomas Vincent, *The True Christian's Love to the Unseen Christ* (Ligonier, PA: Soli Deo Gloria, 1996), 1–2.
10. Rebecca Skloot, *The Immortal Life of Henrietta Lacks* (New York: Random House, 2009), 56.
11. Whittaker Chambers, *Witness* (New York: Random House, 1952), 16.
12. This conversation is included with other testimonies of deathbed faith at Exploring Christianity, http://www.christianity.co.nz/life_death9.htm, accessed 10/11/2011.

Chapter 4: What Makes Love Extravagant

1. Saundra's story is told by Thomas Lake in the September 17, 2012, issue of *Sports Illustrated*: "The Boy They Couldn't Kill," 59–71.
2. R. Kent Hughes, *Luke: That You May Know the Truth*, 2 vols., Preaching the Word (Wheaton, IL: Crossway, 1998), 1:278.
3. Jonathan Edwards, *Religious Affections*, ed. John Smith, vol. 2 of *The Works of Jonathan Edwards* (New Haven, CT: Yale University Press, 1959), 348–49.
4. Quoted by Arnold Dallimore in *George Whitefield*, 2 vols. (Edinburgh: Banner of Truth, 1975), 1:132.
5. John Newton, quoted in Steve Turner, *Amazing Grace: The Story of America's Most Beloved Song* (New York: HarperCollins, 2002), 110.

Chapter 5: What Love Does

1. Alexander Maclaren, *Gospel of St. John*, in *Expositions of Holy Scripture*, vol. 7 (Grand Rapids, MI: Eerdmans, 1959), 315.
2. R. C. Sproul, *John*, St. Andrew's Expositional Commentary (Orlando, FL: Reformation Trust, 2009), 271.
3. David Watson, quoted in Jerry Trousdale, *Miraculous Movements: How Hundreds of Thousands of Muslims Are Falling in Love with Jesus* (Nashville, TN: Thomas Nelson, 2012), 99.
4. Cyril of Alexandria, "Commentary on the Gospel of John,"

Ancient Christian Commentary on Scripture, New Testament IVb: John 11–21, ed. Joel C. Elowsky (Downers Grove, IL: Inter-Varsity, 2007), 137.

Chapter 7: When I Don't Love Jesus

1. James Montgomery Boice recounts this story in *John: An Expositional Commentary*, 5 vols. (Grand Rapids, MI: Baker, 2005), 4:1110.
2. Thomas Vincent, *The True Christian's Love to the Unseen Christ* (Ligonier, PA: Soli Deo Gloria, 1996), 2.
3. Nick Perrin, *Jesus the Temple* (Grand Rapids, MI: Baker, 2010), 127.
4. This story is recounted by Randy C. Alcorn in *Money, Possessions, and Eternity* (Wheaton, IL: Tyndale, 2003), 159.
5. Christopher Lasch, *The Culture of Narcissism: American Life in an Age of Diminished Expectations*, rev. ed. (New York: Norton, 1991), 239.
6. C. S. Lewis, quoted in Armand M. Nicholi, *The Question of God: C. S. Lewis and Sigmund Freud Debate God, Love, Sex, and the Meaning of Life* (New York: Free Press, 2002), 81.
7. J. C. Ryle, *Expository Thoughts on Luke*, 2 vols. (1858; repr. Edinburgh: Banner of Truth, 2012), 2:203.
8. R. Kent Hughes makes a similar point in *Luke: That You May Know the Truth*, 2 vols., Preaching the Word (Wheaton, IL: Crossway, 1998), 2:208.
9. As recounted in Boice, *John*, 1110.

Chapter 8: Sight Unseen

1. Tanya M. Luhrmann, *When God Talks Back: Understanding the American Evangelical Relationship with God*, quoted in Don Troop, "Tuning in to the Voice of God," *The Chronicle Review* (March 30, 2002): B13.
2. Ibid.
3. Charles Colson and Nancy Pearcey, *How Now Shall We Live?* (Wheaton, IL: Tyndale, 1999), 31.
4. Andrew Gray, *Loving Christ and Fleeing Temptation*, ed. Joel R.

Beeke and Kelly Van Wyck (Grand Rapids, MI: Reformation Heritage Books, 2007), 127.

5. Thomas Vincent, *The True Christian's Love for the Unseen Christ* (Ligonier, PA: Soli Deo Gloria, 1996).

6. Thomas Boston, *Human Nature in Its Fourfold State* (Edinburgh: Banner of Truth, 1989), 282–83.

7. Billy Graham, quoted in Laura Hillenbrand, *Unbroken: A World War II Story of Survival, Resilience, and Redemption* (New York: Random House, 2010), 374.

8. Hillenbrand, *Unbroken*, 375.

9. Svetlana Ivanova, from Orlando Figes, *Just Send Me Word: A True Story of Love and Survival in the Gulag*, as quoted in Michael Scammell, "Love Against All Odds," *New York Review of Books* (June 21, 2012): 6.

10. Boston, *Human Nature in Its Fourfold State*, 446.

11. Lizzie Alldridge, *Florence Nightingale, Frances Ridley Havergal, Catherine Marsh, Mrs. Ranyard*, 3rd ed. (New York: Cassel and Company, 1887), 64.

Chapter 9: Loving Jesus Perfectly

1. Kent Crockett, *Making Today Count for Eternity* (Sisters, OR: Multnomah, 2001), 101–2.

2. Frank Thielman provides a helpful survey of interpretive options in *Ephesians*, Baker Exegetical Commentary on the New Testament (Grand Rapids, MI: Baker Academic, 2010), 443–49.

3. Thomas Vincent, *The True Christian's Love to the Unseen Christ* (Ligonier, PA: Soli Deo Gloria, 1996), 31.

4. Thomas Cranmer, "Collect for Purity," *Book of Common Prayer* (1549).

5. Augustine, *De Correptione et Gratia*, ed. J. P. Migne, Patrologiae Cursus Completus, Series Latina, 44 (Paris, 1863), cols. 915–46.

6. Vincent, *True Christian's Love to the Unseen Christ*, 129.

7. Ibid., 10–12.

8. Ibid., 75.

9. This story was written and verified with Lap Vi Ho by our mutual friend Greg Campbell.

Study Guide

1. Jonathan Edwards, *Jonathan Edwards: Representative Selections, with Introduction, Bibliography, and Notes*, rev. ed., ed. C. H. Faust and T. H. Johnson, American Century series (New York: Hill and Wang, 1962), 378.
2. John Piper and D. A. Carson, *The Pastor as Scholar and the Scholar as Pastor: Reflections on Life and Ministry* (Wheaton, IL: Crossway, 2011), 50.
3. John Piper, *Think: The Life of the Mind and the Love of God* (Wheaton, IL: Crossway, 2010), 15.
4. Keith Green, "My Eyes Are Dry, My Faith Is Old," Birdwing Music/Cherry Lane Publishing, 1978.

General Index

spiritual doubts, 33; as a struggle to be acknowledged, 32; as a temptation to be resisted, 32

duchess who rejected an invitation to hear George Whitefield, 70–71

Dudley-Smith, Timothy, 21–22

Dyke, William Montague, 131–32

Edwards, Jonathan, 21, 69, 148

Ephesus, church in, 16, 17

eternal life, 56–57, 111, 123, 134

Faraday, Michael, 38–39

father of the son with an evil spirit, the, 32, 33–34

Fiddler on the Roof, 73–74

First and Greatest Commandment, 44–46, 51, 74

forgiveness, 60, 67–71

Francis of Assisi, 70

glorification, 139

God: as love, 14, 19; love of, 14, 19, 99–100; self-styling of himself as a wounded lover, 16

gospel, the, going back to for the assurance of God's love, 34–36, 37, 102

Graham, Billy, 125

Gray, Andrew, 121

Green, Keith, 156

Havergal, Frances, 130

Havergal, Maria, 130

hedonism, 108

Holy Spirit, the: as the channel of God's love, 19–22, 23, 25, 28, 74, 101, 122; following the inner leading of, 26; grieving of, 27; keeping in step with, 25–28; as the power of obedience for a life of Christlike love, 76; quenching of, 26, 27; shyness of, 24–25; the sign of his presence (faith in Jesus), 23–25

Hosea, 16

Howard, Evan B., 47

Hughes, R. Kent, 64–65, 164n8

Immortal Life of Henrietta Lacks, The (Skloot), 53

In the Beauty of the Lilies (Updike), 31

Ivanova, Svetlana, 126–27

Jesus: Christians' denial of, 93–94; in Christmas carols, 37; crucifixion of, 38, 84, 90; eternal love of, 56–57; in Gethsemane, 55, 88; his loving us with all *his* mind, 51–55, 74; importance of worship in the synagogue or temple to, 97; incarnation of, 90; love of, 36–39, 84–85, 88, 112–13; obedience of,

Scripture Index

Also Available from Phil Ryken

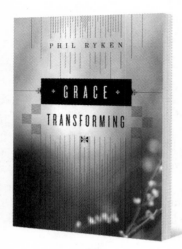

"I so appreciate Ryken's extraordinary insights. . . . If you are seeking a fresh look at your Lord and your own desperate need of him, this is the book for you!"

JONI EARECKSON TADA
Founder and CEO, Joni and Friends International Disability Center

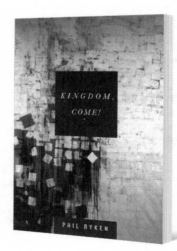

"I absolutely love this book! I have over a hundred books on the Kingdom of God in my library, but this is the only one I'd recommend to everyone."

RICK WARREN
#1 *New York Times* best-selling author, *The Purpose Driven Life*; Pastor, Saddleback Church

For more information, visit crossway.org.